We Can Do This!

Student Mentor Texts

THAT TEACH AND INSPIRE

Janiel Wagstaff

Routledge
Taylor & Francis Group

NEW YORK AND LONDON

A Stenhouse Book

DEDICATION:

For little writers everywhere: Let your big voices be heard!

ACKNOWLEDGMENTS:

Thanks to my family, my school family, and all the student writers
who made contributions. Thanks, too, to SDE, my editor, Tom Schiele,

and designer, Eva Ruutopõld, for their dedicated work!

First published 2017 by Stenhouse Publishers

Published in 2024 by Routledge
605 Third Avenue, New York, NY 10017
4 Park Square, Milton Park, Abingdon, Oxon OX14 4RN

Routledge is an imprint of the Taylor & Francis Group, an informa business

Book design: Eva Ruutopõld

ISBN: 978-1-62531-180-1 (pbk)
ISBN: 978-1-03-268298-3 (ebk)

Table of Contents

★ OTHER TEXT TYPES

★ NOTES

Fixer-Uppers

★ GENERAL GUIDELINES

Introduction

★ Recently, I walked into a fifth-grade classroom with a first grader's story in my hand.

I read a bit of it aloud (it was a fantasy called "The Sea Buddies"). Then, using the document camera, I pointed out several instances of specific word choice. This little writer had included vivid verbs like *deflate*, *bolt*, and *grumble* and imaginative descriptions like, "They all played fin tag and puffer fish tennis in the open sea." The impact on this class of fifth graders was exciting to watch. It was like a mini-writing revolution! "Well, if a first grader can do it, we can definitely do it, too!" Eyes pored over drafts with laser focus. Sure enough, before long the students were talking about the changes they made to *their* verbs and descriptions, eagerly wanting to share their own examples under the document camera.

The power of peer models is undeniable. I've been a happy witness to this under-utilized resource for years. When students see others like themselves taking risks in their writing, persevering, problem-solving, crafting, and succeeding, they become empowered more so than I see with trade mentor texts, anchor charts, or other tools for teaching writing. The models reassure them that they, too, are writers with important ideas to share and the ability to write well. They, too, can do this.

In this book, you're holding a resource rich with the hearts, minds, words, and work of 33 young writers. These pieces are hot-off-their-pencils, *95 percent of them from my Title I school.* Though the precious samples included here were collected over the course of less than a year, they represent a lifetime of passion. My heart and soul is with K–2 writers. I love watching youngsters develop their voices and discover the joy and power of writing. I love to watch kids who can barely scribble a letter of their names blossom into confident page-fillers bursting with ideas to share, armed with the capacity to get the job done. As a K–6 literacy coach, I've worked with our faculty to ensure our students are writing up a storm daily. Though the majority of them entered as kindergartners without the ability to write their names or identify letters, we see the same success story over and over again: Students routinely become successful, motivated writers—not just for standards, but for real purposes.

The movement to use children's trade books as mentor texts for writing instruction has been in full swing for many years. Indeed, professionally authored mentor texts are an instructional staple in writing classrooms, enabling teachers to tune students in to the sound and structure of language and the purpose of varied text types (in addition to just plain getting lost in great literature or building a sense of wonder around well-written exposition). I use them routinely to make specific teaching points and inspire writers across genres. When we couple this resource with peer models that demonstrate attainable results, we get tremendous payback for our investment.

The samples I've chosen to include here are by no means perfect, and they weren't meant to be. We don't want to discourage students by using peer models that seem out of reach. In fact, new research coming out of Harvard and the University of California, Berkeley, demonstrates how the use of *exemplary* peer writing models actually deters students, causing them to be less engaged and even give up (Rogers and Feller, 2016). Naturally, this research has implications for the use of our own students' texts as models. I don't wait around for the perfect example. Instead, I peruse students' writing, both during classroom writing time as they write and during my prep times, looking for teaching points based on needs I see. Then, I choose a student's piece that demonstrates a targeted skill, strategy, element, or craft move that is beginning to develop or is otherwise present. I zero in, celebrating specific attributes in the piece, explaining and defining, typically with the student-author right beside me contributing to the lesson. To put it simply, we mine each other's pieces for parts we can use. We learn from each other, engaged in one another's processes, excited by possibility as we work toward goals. Again, it's not about perfection, but about targeted instruction within the meaningful context of one another's ongoing work. The use of peer models adds to the sense of community in our writing classroom, helping everyone realize we are all teachers and validating each child in the process.

I've been teaching writing for over 27 years. Though every class is different and teaching writing is an exhilarating journey that always promises surprise along the way, I've noticed the same issues come up over and over again. The fact that similar teaching points need to be made year after year is another reason I decided to write this book. Here, you have samples you can use to explicitly name, define, explain, and model these points within an influential, authentic context—that of a peer's writing.

You'll find I emphasize purposefulness in our writing, sharing several samples that were written to serve authentic purposes and audiences. It is my hope that the principle of making writing as purposeful and relevant as possible becomes foundational in the experiences you offer your young writers, as well.

Features at a Glance

The text type

12

Informative

★ **FOCUS:** Naming and supplying information about a topic; staying focused on the topic; revising to add a detail

STANDARDS CONNECTION: Writing informative pieces; naming the topic; supplying information relative to the topic

Here you see the teacher's instructional focus as the text was produced.

Standards are highlighted up front.

Here's an overview of how the mentor text was produced.

INSTRUCTIONAL CONTEXT: Through shared reading, students enjoyed an informative book about frogs. Afterward, the teacher asked them to write about something they learned. Once students finished, she asked them to go back and revise their writing, adding a detail about what they had learned. They used a simple strategy to generate details: reread their pieces and then ask a Who, What, Why, Where, When, or How question. This was modeled several times under the document camera and students paired up to reread and ask a question. After answering, they added their detail to their writing (often by taping on an additional piece of paper).

You can use this mentor text to explicitly make these teaching points.

TEACHING POINTS:

■ Explicitly name the topic and supply information about that topic when writing informative pieces. We stay on topic throughout our piece.

■ Add details by asking simple Who, What, Why, Where, When, or How questions to help our readers learn more about our topic.

IN THIS TEXT:

Claire directly names her topic (frogs) and supplies some information about them, staying true to the topic.

Examples from the mentor text are set in blue italics.

Frogs can hop.

They have web feet.

WRITERS MIGHT CONSIDER:

Ideas for guided practice — getting writers to try out teaching points — are detailed here.

Notice how Claire stayed true to her topic, frogs. Some writers lose sight of their focus and drift off topic. They actually end up writing about something else. Has this ever happened to you? Be sure to always reread your piece to make sure you stay on topic!

What if Claire had written:

Frog can hop. They have web feet. Other animals have web feet, too, like ducks. Ducks swim in water.

Where did Claire go off-topic? Why do you think that happened?

IN THIS TEXT:

Claire added a detail to her piece after her partner asked her Why? (Why do they have webbed feet?). Since she had already used all the space on her paper, she taped on another piece to make the addition.

They use the web feet to swim.

WRITERS MIGHT CONSIDER:

Adding details is not difficult to do. Rereading your piece to your neighbor, asking him to chime in with Who, What, Why, Where, When, or How questions really works. Try it! Partner with another writer. As you listen to his piece, find a place to ask one of these questions. If your partner can answer, he can add a detail to his writing. If he can't answer, he has something to investigate! Now, it's your turn! After you read, your partner asks you a question, and you add a detail to your writing. What do you think? Did this improve your piece?

When more information is available, it is noted here.

To read more about this strategy on a more advanced scale, see Caden's narrative example on page 62.

Hooray! Here's who wrote this piece.

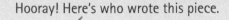

For a reproducible version of this text, see page 108.   *We Can Do This!* 13

AUTHOR:
Claire
GRADE:
K

The mentor texts are included here for easy reference. The full texts are reproduced at the back of the book and are also available online at www.sde.com/mentortexts.

Frogs can hop. They have web feet. They use the web feet to swim.

A transcript of the student text is provided here.

FOLLOW-UP TEACHING:

You will find suggestions on how to extend and expand the mentor text lesson here.

Asking Who, What, Why, Where, When, and How questions is the first strategy I teach throughout the grades to help students add details to their writing. It's simple, and, with some modeling, most students can do it with ease. I keep a list of these questions so children can reference it when working with partners. After they've worked with partners several times, they start internalizing this strategy and can ask themselves questions as they reread. Also, to ensure student understanding, be sure to model asking these questions aloud to yourself as you revise to add details to your writing. Before you know it, you'll see and hear students using the strategy independently!

CYCLE OF ENGAGEMENT

There is a definite cycle of engagement that goes along with using these texts. *First*, you'll see a need in your students' writing or you'll have the need to teach a particular objective based on standards. Use the Matrix of Teaching Points to find a sample that fits that need. *Next*, share the text with your writers. Name the skill or strategy, define it clearly, and point out how the author used it and why. *Follow this* by asking students to try out what they've learned. Ideas for this kind of follow-up are included with the teaching points in the Writers Might Consider sections found in each mentor text. *Then*, debrief to be sure students understand when, why, and how they will use the skill or strategy.

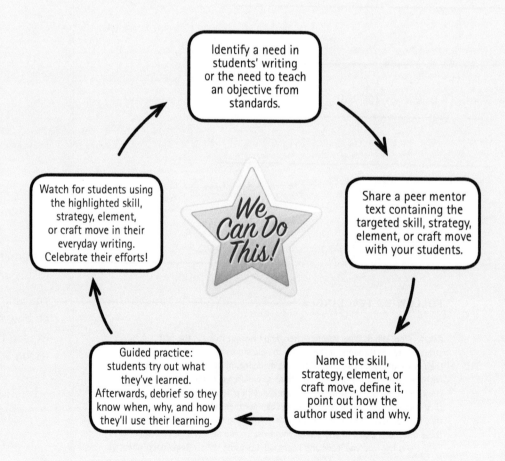

Keep in mind that most teaching points lend themselves to quick, guided practice before students move on to independent writing. For example, one teaching point for Michael's first grade informative piece on black jaguars is to learn to use bold headings. A quick way to practice this after teaching the concept using the mentor text is to read a bit from another informational source and ask students to work in pairs to talk about, and then write, a bold heading that fits that information. Of course, this lesson fits well when students are working on their own informational pieces, so follow up by having them look for categories of information in their writing and compose bold headings to match. *Finally*, look for examples of your students using the skill or strategy in their own writing and celebrate under the document camera. This is HUGELY motivating to writers, and you'll see more and more of what you're looking for when you take the time to include this step.

Teaching from student mentor texts doesn't always have to occur in a whole-group setting. You may find that a particular group of students is in need of a teaching point that the majority of students are not. Pull them aside and conduct a small-group meeting, using the sample to teach just as you would with the whole group.

TEACHING-POINT MATRIX

To facilitate your ability to quickly pinpoint which student mentor text fits your needs at any given time, I've generated a matrix of teaching points included on pages 104–105. Among the teaching points you'll find a focus on:

- teaching the elements and organization of varied text types
- writing processes like generating ideas, prewriting, getting thoughts down on paper for the more emergent to the more fluent writer, revision, and editing
- incorporating craft elements like word choice, sentence structure, and voice into writing
- conventions and spelling

EFFECTIVELY USING THE MENTOR TEXTS

I began this introduction with a story of how I successfully used one first grader's narrative in a fifth-grade classroom. Though there are grade levels attached to the samples, use them flexibly. If it fits your students' needs, use a kindergarten sample in first grade or a second-grade sample in kindergarten. Along these same lines, any sample can be used to make teaching points other than those I've chosen to identify. You may see something differently than I did, or a piece may be the perfect fit for a completely different need.

Focus on one or two teaching points at a time so as to keep lessons short, and save the majority of class time for actual writing. It is perfectly fine to use a mentor text in more than one lesson. In fact, you'll find that's pretty imperative. Teaching points have to be repeated several times for them to stick. And, you'll want to augment the use of these samples with those of your students as you process and celebrate their efforts.

USING YOUR OWN STUDENTS' WRITING AS MENTOR TEXTS

As you use your own students' pieces as mentors, remember to honor the writing of students at varied proficiency levels. We can all learn something from another writer if we look at their writing through a positive lens, even if we highlight just a word or phrase. (Ask yourself, "What has the writer done well here?") Talking publicly with writers at different stages can shed light on strategies they use that may help push others forward. Making writers feel valued is a core reason we use student samples as mentors.

When you find samples that fit particular teaching points, be sure to keep copies for your files. Like me, I'm sure you'll discover similar needs pop up year after year, so you can always use a sample again with a different group of students. And since a particular point often warrants revisiting, if you keep the samples you find valuable, you'll have them ready to go.

NOTES

There's a section of notes at the end of the book that includes quick strategies for fixing up some of the common issues we find in K–2 writing and that you certainly see in the mentor texts here. For example, how do we boost students' abilities to use high-frequency words correctly in their everyday writing (one of my pet peeves)? Or, how do we get them to use writing conventions consistently? Additionally, there are notes about general issues related to working with young writers that I thought you'd find helpful.

A FINAL WORD

I want to personally thank you for taking on the job of developing the abilities and writing lives of young people. Just as we take pride and joy in all we do to build lifelong, proficient readers, the gifts we give students as we scaffold their writing are numerous and far-reaching. We can't possibly imagine where our influence might lead them. I know I want my students to first and foremost love to write and see the value of writing. I want them to want to write, to need to write. This only happens when we write with them daily, struggling through the process side-by-side, celebrating the outcomes. It happens in earnest when we write for relevant, real purposes, beyond tests, and beyond mere schoolish assignments. There's a whole world of joyful writing to relish with students. I hope these mentor texts help you along the way.

I take dance at Jazz
I dance on Mondays and
I take Tap Hip hop
and Acro. I like
In tap class I
Miss Mary teash
shufle and to
change.
Mirs Carly teashes
she takes counts we
the counts. Mri Mu
teaches. Hip hop. to
Acro is streching
I can do a tr
And Jazz is stre
doing a dance, I lik

Student Mentor Texts
INFORMATIVE

Informative

★ **FOCUS:** Naming and supplying information about a topic; staying focused on the topic; revising to add a detail

STANDARDS CONNECTION: Writing informative pieces; naming the topic; supplying information relative to the topic

INSTRUCTIONAL CONTEXT: Through shared reading, students enjoyed an informative book about frogs. Afterward, the teacher asked them to write about something they learned. Once students finished, she asked them to go back and revise their writing, adding a detail about what they had learned. They used a simple strategy to generate details: reread their pieces and then ask a Who, What, Why, Where, When, or How question. This was modeled several times under the document camera and students paired up to reread and ask a question. After answering, they added their detail to their writing (often by taping on an additional piece of paper).

TEACHING POINTS:

■ Explicitly name the topic and supply information about that topic when writing informative pieces. We stay on topic throughout our piece.

■ Add details by asking simple Who, What, Why, Where, When, or How questions to help our readers learn more about our topic.

IN THIS TEXT:

Claire directly names her topic (frogs) and supplies some information about them, staying true to the topic.

> *Frogs can hop.*
>
> *They have web feet.*

WRITERS MIGHT CONSIDER:

Notice how Claire stayed true to her topic, frogs. Some writers lose sight of their focus and drift off topic. They actually end up writing about something else. Has this ever happened to you? Be sure to always reread your piece to make sure you stay on topic!

What if Claire had written:

Frog can hop. They have web feet. Other animals have web feet, too, like ducks. Ducks swim in water.

Where did Claire go off-topic? Why do you think that happened?

IN THIS TEXT:

Claire added a detail to her piece after her partner asked her Why? (Why do they have webbed feet?). Since she had already used all the space on her paper, she taped on another piece to make the addition.

> *They use the web feet to swim.*

WRITERS MIGHT CONSIDER:

Adding details is not difficult to do. Rereading your piece to your neighbor, asking him to chime in with Who, What, Why, Where, When, or How questions really works. Try it! Partner with another writer. As you listen to his piece, find a place to ask one of these questions. If your partner can answer, he can add a detail to his writing. If he can't answer, he has something to investigate! Now, it's your turn! After you read, your partner asks you a question, and you add a detail to your writing. What do you think? Did this improve your piece?

To read more about this strategy on a more advanced scale, see Caden's narrative example on page 62.

AUTHOR:
Claire

GRADE:
K

Frogs can hop. They have web feet. They use the web feet to swim.

FOLLOW-UP TEACHING:

Asking Who, What, Why, Where, When, and How questions is the first strategy I teach throughout the grades to help students add details to their writing. It's simple, and, with some modeling, most students can do it with ease. I keep a list of these questions so children can reference it when working with partners. After they've worked with partners several times, they start internalizing this strategy and can ask themselves questions as they reread. Also, to ensure student understanding, be sure to model asking these questions aloud to yourself as you revise to add details to your writing. Before you know it, you'll see and hear students using the strategy independently!

Informative

★ **FOCUS:** Beginning writing with a topic phrase or sentence that allows the reader to know just what you will be sharing; staying laser-focused on a tight topic in a short piece

STANDARDS CONNECTION: Participating in shared research and writing projects

INSTRUCTIONAL CONTEXT: In the story *My Garden* by Kevin Henkes, a young girl plants seeds along with many other interesting things in her garden, such as sea shells and chocolate chips. To her delight, everything she plants grows. After reading this fictional tale, students wondered what really does grow, so they conducted experiments mimicking what the girl planted. They observed their plantings over many weeks, writing about what they were noticing. Finally, I asked them to draw conclusions about what they had learned.

TEACHING POINTS:

- Begin your writing with words that tell your reader exactly what you'll be sharing.
- Our topic is very focused. We're not repeating what we've already written about our experiments. Instead we are drawing conclusions about what we've learned. Stay focused on only that topic in a short piece.

IN THIS TEXT:

Cale uses an opening phrase that directly tells her reader what she'll be sharing:

> *I learned that...*

WRITERS MIGHT CONSIDER:

What are some additional ways Cale might have started her piece so readers would know exactly what she was writing about? I wonder if she may have included a bit more information for her reader. For example, how did she learn the information?

What if she had written:

> *The plant experiments taught me...*

or

> *Because we planted many different things, I now know...*

Have students try different variations of her statement aloud including more details. Relate this to a topic you've already studied. For example, *Our study of Martin Luther King Jr. taught me...*

IN THIS TEXT:

Cale stays laser-focused on the tight topic. The big idea from the experiments was that

> *only seeds grow.*

WRITERS MIGHT CONSIDER:

What other big conclusions have you come to in your learning? (Assist students in thinking of some examples from recent studies.) How might these sound if they were stated with focus in a short piece?

AUTHOR:
Cale

GRADE:
K

Cale / /

I lrnd that only seds gro.

I learned that only seeds grow.

FOLLOW-UP TEACHING:

I suggest doing quick, focused writing like this to sum up learning, data, or findings for any experiment or unit of study. This is a very different kind of writing and thinking, especially when you are pushing students to higher levels of thinking by asking them to grasp and communicate the big picture. If the majority of your students are struggling, talk it through together and record the final, focused idea with shared or interactive writing. Repeat, repeat, repeat! This is purposeful, integrated, cross-curricular writing. Don't be discouraged; students' abilities will grow with experience. Work like this will help prepare them for topic-sentence writing when they're older.

Informative/Explanatory

★ **FOCUS:** Clearly introducing the topic; organizing information around main ideas or categories

STANDARDS CONNECTION: Informative/Explanatory writing: supplying facts

INSTRUCTIONAL CONTEXT: Students wrote about a hobby as the teacher modeled writing about hers. They were asked to name the hobby and include relevant details in at least two categories. The teacher provided a model by writing her piece around two categories (or main ideas): her beads and the types of jewelry she makes. "I have all kinds of beads I use to make jewelry. I have metal beads, beads made of wood, and beads made of plastic. There is a variety of colors. I make different types of jewelry with my beads. I make necklaces and bracelets. Earrings are also fun to make."

TEACHING POINTS:
- Name your topic (hobby) and explain where and when you participate in it.
- Organize the details about your hobby around main ideas or categories of ideas. Include at least two categories of information.

IN THIS TEXT:

Katelyn names her hobby and explains where and when she participates in it. She has very clear details.

I take dance at Jazz Dancer Studio.
She names her hobby and where she engages in it.

I dance on Mondays and Thursdays.
She states what days of the week she dances.

WRITERS MIGHT CONSIDER:

Why would writers want to name their hobby very close to the beginning of their piece? Why include the details of where and when you participate in a hobby? What hobbies do you like? Can you name these details?

IN THIS TEXT:

Katelyn organizes her writing around each of the different types of dance lessons she takes:

- *In tap class, I wear tap shoes. Miss Mary teaches us to shuffle and to kick ball change.*
- *Miss Carly teaches hip hop. She takes counts. We dance to counts. Mr. Murphy, he teaches hip hop, too.*
- *Acro is stretching and tumbling. I can do a backbend!*
- *And, jazz is stretching and doing a dance.*

WRITERS MIGHT CONSIDER:

What do you think of the way Katelyn organized her writing? Does it make sense? I wonder if there are other ways to organize writing about a hobby?

For a reproducible version of this text, see page 110.

AUTHOR:
Katelyn
GRADE:
1

Katelyn

I take dance at Jazz Dancer Studio. I dance on Mondays and Thursdays. I take tap, hip-hop, jazz and acro. I like to dance! In tap class I wear tap shoes. Miss Mary teaches us to shuffle and to kick-ball-change. Miss Carly teaches hip-hop. She takes counts. We dance to the counts. Mr. Murphy, he teaches hip-hop, too. Acro is stretching and tumbling. I can do a back bend! And, jazz is stretching and doing a dance. I like dance!

FOLLOW-UP TEACHING:

Model writing your own piece about a hobby. Consider using bold headings to break up the sections (see Michael's informative piece on page 18. This type of writing could also be organized procedurally, step-by-step (see Hailey's text on page 20). I enjoy writing about hobbies with children because exploring this topic is another way for us to learn more about each other.

Informative

★ **FOCUS:** Using informative text features: bold headings and diagrams

STANDARDS CONNECTION: Writing informative pieces; knowing the effects of various text features and how to use them

INSTRUCTIONAL CONTEXT: Students chose an animal to investigate. With guidance from the teacher, they used sources to look for a limited amount of specific information: where the animal lives and what the animal looks like. Following the teacher's model, students chunked the text, writing it piece by piece, labeling sections with bold headings. They finished by adding a diagram. (These were features they had previously studied while *reading* informative texts.)

TEACHING POINTS:
- Chunk text into main ideas about your topic. Use bold headings to label each main idea and let the reader know what to expect in the following section.
- Use diagrams to accurately and precisely draw and label specific parts of the subject under study. Visuals like this deepen readers' understanding.

IN THIS TEXT:

Michael uses bold headings to introduce each of his sections. He traced the words and underlined them to make them stand out.

- *Habitat*
- *Looks*

WRITERS MIGHT CONSIDER:

As I gather information about a topic, I need to stay focused and organized. I can't learn everything about my topic; I have to narrow what I'm looking for. What are the main ideas or main questions I'm investigating? Can I use bold headings to make these clear to my readers? If so, what might those headings be? (Students might work with the teacher to gather a list of bold headings related to topics they're investigating. These could be lifted directly from other informative texts and used to stimulate ideas as students work on developing questions, researching, and chunking the text into sections while writing about their own topics.)

IN THIS TEXT:

Michael includes a diagram, labeling important features of the black jaguar.

- *black fur*
- *sharp claws*
- *big eyes*
- *long tail*

WRITERS MIGHT CONSIDER:

In addition to the specific labels in the diagram, sometimes authors and illustrators include a small bit of important information:

- *black fur* (for camouflage)
- *sharp claws* (to kill prey)
- *big eyes* (to hunt at night)
- *long tail* (for balance)

Black Jaguar

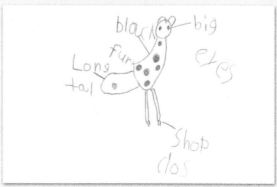

big eyes   black fur   long tail   sharp claws

AUTHOR:
Michael
GRADE:
1

Name: Michael G

Habitat: South
America.
ther are a lot
of trees.
Its warem.
ther are dens.

Looks:
The black
jagwor has
black fre.
The back Jagwor
has black
spos.
I chose the
black jackware
been those they

Habitat: South America. There are a lot of trees. It's warm. There are dens.

Looks: The black jaguar has black fur. The black jaguar has black spots. I chose the black jaguar because they can blend in the shadows.

FOLLOW-UP TEACHING:

Animals are always a popular topic for informative writing with young students. But what are their other unique interests? Keep a Running Topic List (Wagstaff, 2011) of ideas that come up during conversation. Invite students to investigate these topics, determining a few main ideas or questions to research, keeping brief notes, chunking the text to write about each section, and using text features they've studied and used in the past. My picture book, *Stella and Class: Information Experts*, is a great resource for stimulating students' thinking about their own topics and teaching them how to investigate topics.

Informative/Procedural

★ **FOCUS:** Organizing ideas in logical ways, using temporal words

STANDARDS CONNECTION: Informative/Procedural writing

INSTRUCTIONAL CONTEXT: Procedural writing is always engaging! We often use shared writing to write about classroom experiences and experiments, learning how to attend to details in sequence. For this piece, students wrote procedural information about something they like to do outside of class, focusing on the use of temporal words to organize their writing.

TEACHING POINTS:

■ Name your topic. What is it you like to do?

■ Give step-by-step details about how to do it using temporal words: first, second, third or first, next, then, last.

IN THIS TEXT:

Hailey names her topic and includes details about when she engages in this procedure and with whom.

> *What I do in the winter I build a snowman…*

She names the topic and when she engages in it.

> *a girl snowman…*

She gets even more specific, telling us she builds female snowmen!

> *with my dad.*

She includes who she works with.

WRITERS MIGHT CONSIDER:

Play with the organization of Hailey's first sentence. Change the order of the words. What is another way to structure that sentence?

IN THIS TEXT:

Hailey organizes her writing with a step-by-step explanation, using the words first, second, and third:

- *First, we put snow for her body.*

- *Second, we put a carrot for her nose, and we put buttons for her eyes.*

- *Third, we put a hat on the snowman.*

WRITERS MIGHT CONSIDER:

What detail does Hailey include in her picture that she does not include in her text (the snowgirl has stick arms). If she was to add that detail in, where would it go? What temporal word might be used with this addition? Is another temporal word necessary?

AUTHOR:
Hailey
GRADE:
1

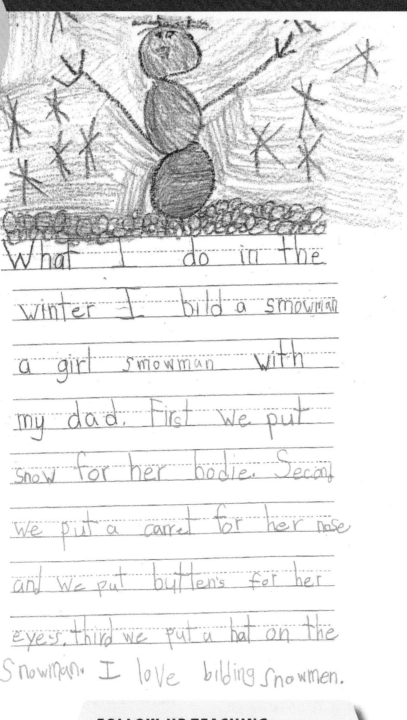

What I do in the winter I build a snowman, a girl snowman with my dad. First we put snow for her body. Second we put a carrot for her nose and we put buttons for her eyes. Third we put a hat on the snowman. I love making snowmen!

What I do in the winter I bild a smowman a girl smowman with my dad. First we put snow for her bodie. Secont we put a carret for her nose and we put buttens for her eyess. third we put a hat on the Snowman. I love bilding snowmen.

FOLLOW-UP TEACHING:

How-tos are great fun and make perfect contexts for teaching about the importance of organization. Share some how-to books and examine how they are organized. Copy pages from the books that show different organizational schemes. Tape them to a chart and label them. Model writing your own how-to text, using one of the organizational ideas represented. Invite children to do the same.

Another follow-up idea is to write a procedural piece about something your class does at school, such as getting ready for dismissal. Write the piece as a non-example, mixing up the steps, lacking organization. Work with your class to reorganize the piece, putting in temporal words. Debrief about what you did and why!

Procedural

★ **FOCUS:** Editing and organization

STANDARDS CONNECTION: Writing procedural pieces; editing for conventions and mechanics

INSTRUCTIONAL CONTEXT: Students wrote a procedural piece about the steps they take when doing something fun with a family member. To help with organization, they planned the writing in Thinking Boxes labeled First, Next, Then, and Last, and talked-it-out (see Ruby's narrative piece on page 58). After writing, they went back to edit using the Circle Things We Know strategy (Wagstaff 2011, 2016).

TEACHING POINTS:
■ When writing about procedures, plan and then record the steps in order so your reader can understand exactly what you do step-by-step.
■ Edit your writing for the conventions and mechanics you know using the Circle Things We Know strategy.

IN THIS TEXT:

Lucio planned his piece in Thinking Boxes, but when he wrote it, he did not include the temporal words. He was still able to organize his steps in order by working from the graphic organizer:

We get the buns and patties.
Here is what he does first.

We put them on the grill.
This is his next step.

We take them off and put them in the buns.
This is what happens then.

Yum. Let's eat!!!
This is the last step.

WRITERS MIGHT CONSIDER:

Try it! When you plan a piece using temporal words, write it without the words *first, next,* etc., but still in order. Experiment out loud by reading it with and without those words. Which version do you like better?

IN THIS TEXT:

Lucio went back to his piece to Circle Things He Knows. He spotted several things he did well and made several corrections!

• He circled his first word, *I,* to celebrate something he did well. Notice how you can see he actually fixed the lower case *i* and made it into a capital letter!

• He circled his period at the end of the first sentence and his capital to start the next sentence.

• He found and circled several high-frequency words that he spelled correctly: *the, and, put*

• He circled more end marks and made several corrections to capitals as he went along: He changed the lowercase *w* to uppercase in his third sentence and the lowercase *y* to uppercase in his fourth sentence.

WRITERS MIGHT CONSIDER:

Try it! What do you know about how sentences begin and end? Do you know how to spell high-frequency words? More importantly, do you show these skills every day when you write? Take out a piece of your writing. Go through it carefully, circling the things you know you've done well as a writer. If you find mistakes, you can fix them and circle them. Congratulate yourself on a job well done.

For more on the Circling Things We Know strategy, see pages 95–96.

AUTHOR:
Lucio
GRADE:
1

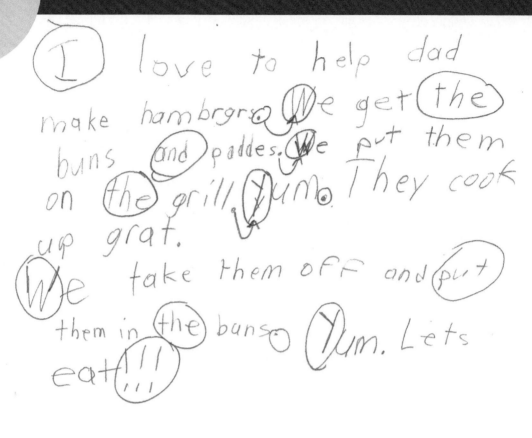

I love to help dad make hamburgers. We get the buns and patties. We put them on the grill. Yum.
They cook up great. We take them off and put them in the buns. Yum. Let's eat!

FOLLOW-UP TEACHING:

The Circling Things We Know strategy is something I came up with years ago
to fix the problem of mechanics in students' writing. It seemed they could tell
you what they knew was right when it came to capitals, periods, and spelling
high-frequency words, but when they actually wrote, it all went out the window.
This is like a magical trick that solves the problem. Students actually want to
look back at their writing when we frame it as Circling Things We Know. That
sounds positive, and they are more than happy to show off their skills (fixing
mistakes along the way, of course!). We celebrate their examples under the
document camera, as always, and we use word walls to help support this process. In particular, we have a Help Wall (see page 95) that reminds students of
mechanics and conventions they know, so when they go back to circle, they have
some support. If you're interested, see *Teaching Reading and Writing with Word
Walls* (Wagstaff, 1999) for a whole chapter on this type of word wall.

Informative

INSTRUCTIONAL CONTEXT: Once word spread that one first grade class read about a student in our school who had completed a service project, the class next door wanted to learn about the same student, what he did, and why. This class and I decided to read and view sources about him so we could write to inform the whole school and spread the word even further. We studied two sources: a newspaper article and a slideshow of photographs, collecting information in three columns: Who, What, and Why. Students used this shared organizer to talk-out their writing. They then composed individual pieces that were shared among classmates. Last, we wrote a shared piece that was enlarged to poster size. We made several copies; students illustrated and labeled them; and we hung them around the school so others could learn about and be inspired by Jack.

TEACHING POINTS:
- Gather information from more than one source to accurately inform others about who Jack is, what he did, and why he did it.
- Include a purposeful conclusion.

IN THIS TEXT:

Ainslee informs readers about who Jack is, what he did, and why using details from our sources:

> *Jack Stevenson was a nice boy.*

She names who, stating Jack's full name.

> *selling snow cones*

She shares what he did

> *helped the police dog, Delta*

and why.

WRITERS MIGHT CONSIDER:

What questions do you have when you read Ainslee's piece? What details about who, what, and why are still missing? (She might have included how old Jack is and that he is part of our school community. I'd also like to know more details about how or when Jack sold the snow cones and for how much. Plus, how was the police dog helped?)

Is there someone inspirational you know who you might spread the word about? You can either interview or research that person to share informative details about who he is, what he did, and why he is noteworthy.

IN THIS TEXT:

Students were asked why they thought we should share Jack's story with the whole school. This question was designed to help them form purposeful conclusions. We discussed how Jack's project could inspire others to do good in our community. This helped Ainslee write a purposeful conclusion:

> *Don't you think you could do something like that?*

WRITERS MIGHT CONSIDER:

When you read an inspiring story or learn something you think others should know, write about it! Then, make sure to include why you thought the story or information should be shared. This will help you come up with a purposeful conclusion. Maybe you can inspire others to do something, make something, change their thinking, or learn more about the world!

AUTHOR:
Ainslee

GRADE:
1

The Nice Boy
Jack Stevenson was
a nice boy. He helpt
the plees dog Delta
by Seling snow cons
because he was nice

unuf to do that.
Dont you thenk you
can do sum thing
like that.

The Nice Boy

Jack Stevenson was a nice boy. He helped the police dog Delta by selling snow cones because he was nice enough to do that. Don't you think you can do something like that?

FOLLOW-UP TEACHING:

It's amazing how using multiple text and digital resources ignites students' enthusiasm for learning. I often put together slideshows of images based on topics we are studying (this is easily accomplished by doing a quick search in Google Images). I show one photo at a time and invite children to talk about what they see and what they wonder. They are great visual investigators, seeing things we adults sometimes miss, and they are highly skilled questioners. Often, I'll show a short video clip as an additional way to bring information to life.

When working on informative pieces with young children, it is best to have them focus on just a few specific questions they can easily answer from the sources. Once their appetite has been whetted, students are more eager to read and study texts, looking for answers to their specific questions. Working from multiple sources gets students excitedly talking, writing, and feeling like real experts!

Informative

★ **FOCUS:** Using a simple graphic organizer to collect and organize information for writing; scaffolding writing by talking-out points from a graphic organizer

STANDARDS CONNECTION: Writing informative text, pulling from several sources

INSTRUCTIONAL CONTEXT: If we hook our writers with interesting and relevant topics, we'll get more quality informative writing. For this piece, we watched video clips from the Internet and read articles about a young boy, Caine Monroy, who created a cardboard arcade out of boxes. His creativity inspired children to use their imaginations to create games out of cardboard, too. People donated to Caine's online college fund and, in turn, inspired him to create a foundation to fund creativity in children and establish a special day called "The Cardboard Challenge" to celebrate creativity around the world. Using their two-column notes, students wrote their pieces in the form of newspaper articles, and we made copies to distribute to our K–6 student body.

TEACHING POINTS:

■ Use a simple two-column notes graphic organizer to keep track of and organize information.

■ Use just key words as we take notes to ensure what we write is in our own words, not copied from sources.

■ Use two-column notes or other graphic organizers to talk-out your writing. Talking-out writing helps you tease out thinking, play with how to best state your points, and prepare to write.

IN THIS TEXT:

Andy uses his two-column notes to organize information around two main ideas: How Caine used his imagination, and how he changed the world:

- *boxes, tape = arcade*

- *summer vacation*

- *games got bigger and better*

Among many other pertinent points, Andy included what Caine did, when he did it, and details about it.

WRITERS MIGHT CONSIDER:

It's so easy to fold a paper and *Voila!* have a handy organizer. We often fold a sheet of paper in half or thirds depending on how many main ideas we're targeting about a topic.

IN THIS TEXT:

Andy used many key words in his notes, thus avoiding copying too much from sources.

Cardboard challenge every October

These key words remind Andy of one of the ways Caine changed the world. He must take these key details and write them out in whole sentences, using his own words.

WRITERS MIGHT CONSIDER:

While looking at a text or other source, use small sticky notes to record one key idea or a few key words for a topic you are studying. How do you determine what the important points and key words are?

IN THIS TEXT:

Andy used his notes to rehearse his writing out loud. This helped him determine how best to record his findings in an appropriate manner for the task, purpose, and audience.

- Andy talked-out his writing in whole sentences. He did this numerous times as he wrote to orally rehearse as he went along.

- He talked-out his piece, one column at a time, helping him determine in which order he'd like to present his points (thus he numbered them).

Then, he wrote about just that first column before going on to the second.

WRITERS MIGHT CONSIDER:

Have you ever talked something out before you wrote it? Did you find this made the task of writing easier? Talking things out, especially once you have brainstormed your thoughts on paper (as when you use a graphic organizer), helps you get your writing down. If you couple this idea with reading and rereading as you write, you'll craft a higher quality piece.

AUTHOR:
Andy
GRADE:
2

First Column: Use Imagination

boxes, tape = arcade
first game mini basketball
summer vacation
fun pass only $2
his games got bigger and better
soccer game and people
said it was too easy
then he made it harder
He made his own shirt.

Second Column: Change the World

Cardboard Challenge
Every October
video Caine wanted people
to make their
own stuff

FOLLOW-UP TEACHING:

I watch for students using these two strategies: focusing on key words and talking-out their writing using their notes or organizers. I call students forward to model for the class how they turn their key words into sentences. This, of course, can only happen after plenty of modeling on my part and class-guided practice. When students hear how their peers create their language in the air, messing up, trying again, restating, then writing, they learn the power of talking-it-out and practice it often independently. For more information on this strategy and to see how our newspaper articles on Caine were developed from start to finish, see *The Common Core Companion: Booster Lessons, Grades K–2* (Wagstaff, 2016).

Informative

★ **FOCUS:** Voice; organization; using content-specific vocabulary

STANDARDS CONNECTION: Informative writing: introducing topic, providing facts and definitions, including closing statement

INSTRUCTIONAL CONTEXT: Students studied severe weather by reading several texts and articles in choice groups. They worked together to take notes as they pulled relevant details from the texts around main ideas. Then they wrote, focusing on employing voice, organization, and including content-specific vocabulary. The teacher modeled parts of the process, on the areas of need specified here, as this was later in the year and students were more skilled.

TEACHING POINTS:
- ■ Use voice to enliven the factual information.
- ▪ Organize your writing in some manner: main ideas and details, question/answer, sequentially.
- ■ Include relevant vocabulary as needed.

IN THIS TEXT:

Adrian uses a great voice to begin his piece, putting the reader right into the scene:

> *Woah! I see a tornado. Aaaahhh! It is going to hit us! It is almost here! Help me!*

Perhaps he overdid it a bit, but you can feel the fear someone might experience if a tornado was near.

WRITERS MIGHT CONSIDER:

Do you like this method for beginning an informative piece? Why?

Try it! Say you're just starting an informative piece on volcanoes. Mirror Adrian's voice by putting your reader right into the scene. What might that sound like?

I also wonder, what is another way Adrian may have started his piece?

IN THIS TEXT:

Adrian used a question-and-answer format for organizing his piece:

> *What do you do when a tornado is here? You find shelter.*

He doesn't stop with a simple one-sentence answer; he provides details:

> *Don't go by windows because it will hurt you!*

Then he asks:

> *What kind of tornados are there? A rope tornado…waterspout tornado…wedge tornado…*

He provides a brief description about each type.

> *What is a tornado? A tornado has lightning. It has rain. It is like a funnel.*

WRITERS MIGHT CONSIDER:

Question-and-answer can be an effective format. What is a topic you'd like to investigate? Would a question-and-answer format work for you? If so, what questions might you pose?

Could Adrian try organizing his sections differently? How? Why? (It makes sense to start the piece with the question: *What is a tornado?* so the reader gets that critical information up front, rather than at the end.)

IN THIS TEXT:

Adrian makes effective use of content-specific vocabulary:

- *A rope tornado is like a rope, and they are skinny.*

- *There's a waterspout tornado; a waterspout is a tornado that can go on water.*

- *A wedge tornado is the biggest tornado.*

WRITERS MIGHT CONSIDER:

What more would you like to know about this content-specific vocabulary? For example, I'd like more details about a wedge tornado. What does one look like? Did you have the same question? What does that mean for your own use of content-specific vocabulary? (Be sure to include details to define the terms you use.)

AUTHOR:
Adrian

GRADE:
2

Tornados

Woah! I see a tornado. Aaaahhh!
It is going to hit us! It is almost here.
Help me! What do you do when a
tornado is here? You find shelter.
Don't go by windows because it will
hurt you! It will destroy houses.

What kinds of tornados are there?
A rope tornado is like a rope and
they are skinny. There's a waterspout
tornado. A waterspout is a tornado
that can go on water. A wedge
tornado is the biggest tornado.

What is a tornado? A tornado has
lightning. It has rain. It is like a
funnel. I don't like tornados because
they destroy everything.

Adrian

Tonadoes

Woah! I see a Tonadoe Aaaaaa! It is ging to hit us. It is omost here! Help Me! Waht do you do wen a tonadoe is here? You find Settter Don't go by Windos because it will hurt You It will destroy houses.

What kinds of tornados are there? A rope tornad is like a rope and they are skinny. Theres a waterspout tonadoe, a waterspout is a tonadoe that can go on water.

FOLLOW-UP TEACHING:

Study other question-and-answer texts. What techniques do authors use to pose questions (bold headings, the first sentence in a section or paragraph, etc.) and provide answers (bulleted lists, detailed paragraphs, diagrams with labels, etc.)?

Study how writers incorporate content-specific vocabulary in their writing. How do they do it? What techniques do they use to define terms to make sure their readers understand (parenthetical information, definitions, or examples between commas, definitions in the following sentences, diagrams with labels, etc.)? You might also notice how some texts use boldface type or italics for vocabulary. Try using these techniques.

Informative

★ **FOCUS:** Starting a piece in an interesting way to capture readers' attention; using varied beginnings for sentences

STANDARDS CONNECTION: Writing informative pieces; author's craft: capturing readers' attention right at the start, varying sentence beginnings

INSTRUCTIONAL CONTEXT: Students chose an animal they wanted to research, focusing attention on three main ideas: habitat, diet, and appearance. As students read, they added specific details to a three-main-idea graphic organizer. After the teacher modeled using three *ing* verbs to begin her piece, the class generated an *ing* verb list about their animals and used this to construct their attention-grabbing opening sentences. Further, as drafting occurred, the teacher modeled using pronouns (among other strategies) to vary the beginnings of her sentences since she noticed, in previous writing, that many students needed to work on this skill.

TEACHING POINTS:

■ Draw readers in with attention-grabbing beginnings. Using three *ing* verbs (Hoyt, 2011) is an example of one of these beginnings.

■ Vary the way sentences begin so the writing doesn't sound repetitive. (In Kinsley's piece, I would call this the "weasel, weasel, weasel" problem.) One simple way to vary beginnings is to use pronouns.

IN THIS TEXT:

Kinsley uses three *ing* verbs to craft her attention-grabbing beginning:

> ***Burrowing, hunting, shedding, weasels are wonderful.***

The three verbs indicate interesting things weasels do and begin the piece with action.

Kinsley even threw in some alliteration as another attention-grabbing element.

WRITERS MIGHT CONSIDER:

What are some additional examples of attention-grabbing beginnings? Mine mentor informative texts to find and list more. Try them out! How do they make your writing sound? How are these types of beginnings useful?

IN THIS TEXT:

Kinsley's draft had a "weasel, weasel, weasel" problem. Almost every sentence in her writing began with the word *weasel*. After revising her work and replacing *weasel* with the pronoun *they*, Kinsley was more able to vary the beginning of her sentences.

> ***They hunt voles, mice, and rabbits, and they also steal eggs from bird's nests.***

This is a sentence she revised, replacing the beginning word Weasels with the pronoun *They*.

> ***Most weasels shed...***

The word *Most* adds some variety.

> ***They turn white!***

Another example of using the proper pronoun. This sentence is also particularly effective because it varies in length from the others (sentence fluency).

WRITERS MIGHT CONSIDER:

In addition to using pronouns to replace nouns and adding number words like *most*, what are other ways to begin sentences to add variety to your writing? Read favorite informative texts with this in mind. List examples of varied, interesting sentence beginnings. Try them and evaluate their effect on your writing.

AUTHOR:
Kinsley
GRADE:
2

Burrowing, hunting, shedding, weasels are wonderful. Weasels live in logs, burrows, and rock piles, too. They hunt voles, mice and rabbits and they also steal eggs from bird nests. Most weasels shed their brown fur to blend in with the snow. They turn white! They go head first with their long bodies into tiny burrows to sleep, live and hunt. They also start to hunt when they are two months old. I want to see a weasel.

Burrowing, hunting, sheding, Weasels are wonderfull. Here are ~~things about them.~~ Weasels live in logs, burrows, and rock piles too. They Weasels hunt voles, mice and rabbits and they also stil eggs from bird nests. Most weasels shed there brown fur to blend in wyth

①

FOLLOW-UP TEACHING:

One of my favorite ways to revisit varied sentence beginnings with students is to write a non-example, using the same beginning throughout (like starting each sentence with the same noun or pronoun or with the word *and*). I show the piece under the document camera and ask for students' reactions. They immediately notice the problem. I model various ways to fix this by rereading and revising. We list some of the strategies they see me model for reference for future writing. (Reminder: this may have to be done several times for it to really stick and make a difference in students' writing.)

I wihs we
have saming
then milk.
becauss m
is gros. ha
with me.

Student Mentor Texts
OPINION

Opinion

INSTRUCTIONAL CONTEXT: The class and I conducted an action-research project, polling other classes about which rule they thought was most important in school and why. We had many occasions to engage in shared writing as we collected data, read, and pondered our question. During this process, students wrote their own opinions about which school rule they thought was most important.

TEACHING POINTS:

- Before writing, talk about what you want to put down on the page. When you write, try to put down letters to match the sounds in the words you said. This helps us grow our writing skills!
- Communicate your thinking through drawing. It is important to include as many details in your picture(s) as you can so readers get the most meaning possible. Details also help you remember what you've written.

IN THIS TEXT:

Gracie's opinion is that the most important school rule is to tell an adult if you see bullying. She shows this in her writing.

At the top of her page, we see

> *B-L-E*

for the word *bully*. Gracie used the Stretchy Hands Strategy to hear a beginning, middle, and ending sound in the word and wrote down a letter for each sound she heard.

She included this word in the speech bubble below, as well. The boy is pointing and yelling

> *BULLY!*

(The other speech bubble says,

> *HA, HA, HA!,*

noting the reaction of the bully.)

WRITERS MIGHT CONSIDER:

Grow your writing skills every day by attempting to caption your pictures like Gracie has at the top of her page. Even if you can't write a whole sentence yet, listening inside even just one word for sounds and then representing these with the letters you know makes you a better speller and builds your writing muscles!

IN THIS TEXT:

Gracie uses an astounding amount of detail in her drawing to express her opinion!

- She sets the scene by including a slide.

- The students show emotion on their faces, helping us understand their feelings. For example, the girl who has been pushed down has a big frown, and the tall girl by the slide looks bewildered and worried.

- Notice the detail of the glasses on the ground. They have either been knocked off the face of the girl who has been pushed down, or she has dropped them.

WRITERS MIGHT CONSIDER:

What additional details do you see that we have not mentioned? What do you think they mean? What can we learn about our own drawings from studying Gracie's?

Look at a picture you have recently drawn. Decide on at least one detail you can add to show more of your opinion, story, or information. Share the detail you added with a neighbor.

For more information about the Stretchy Hands Strategy see page 91.

2122111

AUTHOR: Gracie
GRADE: K

Gracie

BIE N

FOLLOW-UP TEACHING:

Make the idea of segmenting a word to hear its sounds concrete by using a slinky as a model. Slowly segment a word while you stretch the slinky, voicing the beginning, middle, and ending sounds. As students get the idea, I teach them to use their fists to imitate the action of the slinky. We put our two fists together then stretch them apart as we voice the sounds in words. We then connect the sounds to letters, calling this the Stretchy Hands Strategy. Students won't always have a slinky, but they'll always have their hands! The strategy has to be modeled repeatedly and students need guided practice with feedback. Celebrate their logical attempts to use the strategy to caption or add speech bubbles to their illustration(s).

To find out more about the whole integrated instructional sequence focused on rules, see *The Common Core Companion: Booster Lessons, Grades K–2*.

Opinion

⭐ **FOCUS:** Stating one's opinion on a topic with the support of a graphic organizer; presenting one's opinion to an audience

STANDARDS CONNECTION: Writing an opinion; presenting one's writing to an audience (speaking and listening)

INSTRUCTIONAL CONTEXT: As the winter holidays approached, the classroom was abuzz with talk of preparations, traditions, and, of course, presents! We took advantage of the excitement and asked students to consider what would be the best holiday gift they could receive and why. Each child would present her opinion to a group using Thinking Boxes (Wagstaff, 2011, 2016).

TEACHING POINTS:
- Decide your opinion on the topic, but think carefully about your reason(s). Why do you feel the way you do? It isn't enough to just say a giraffe is the best present. We want to know why!
- Plan a presentation by organizing your thinking in a graphic organizer. Thinking Boxes are a great tool to help us think (just one box at a time—very doable!), organize, remember, and present our thinking.

IN THIS TEXT:

Nevaeh writes and quickly sketches what she thinks would be the best present and why, filling in one Thinking Box at a time:

In Thinking Box #1, students wrote the name of and sketched (if they chose) what they thought would be the best present. Nevaeh wrote

Barbie.
(Note the pink lipstick and lush lashes!)

In Thinking Box #2, students stated the reason(s) behind their opinions. Nevaeh wrote
because my sister has a Barbie doll.

WRITERS MIGHT CONSIDER:

Might Nevaeh have told us a bit more about her choice and reason? I'd love to know what kind of Barbie doll she wants. Does she want a Barbie doll so she and her sister can play together?

IN THIS TEXT:

Students were asked to practice presenting their opinion orally several times. As they spoke, they used their Thinking Boxes to remind them of what they wanted to say.

Nevaeh practiced her opinion thoroughly so she was confident when she presented to her group.

WRITERS MIGHT CONSIDER:

What skills are important when speaking to a group? How might having the Thinking Boxes help you?

For more on Thinking Boxes, see pages 58–59.

AUTHOR:
Nevaeh
GRADE:
K

Thinking Box 1: Best gift Barbie   Thinking Box 2: because my sister has a Barbie doll

FOLLOW-UP TEACHING:

We're always sharing our writing, even if the sharing time is a quick three minutes. It's key to being purpose-driven, keeping motivation high, and developing one's writing process. Planning more "formal" presentations is also beneficial so students gain experience speaking in front of a group— all eyes on them. Allowing students to practice first is essential to increase their comfort levels, and having a simple organizer like Thinking Boxes by their side enables them to experience success.

Opinion

INSTRUCTIONAL CONTEXT: As our kindergartners' writing skills flourish, we often see a need to do lessons on spacing. Seems students get moving along so fluidly that all the words cram together. As students constructed their opinions about winter, we asked them to place a Cheerio in between each word to remind them to leave spaces (Kisloski and Feldman, 2015). Another sticking point is end mark punctuation. We use "Stop Spotters" to support students with this skill.

TEACHING POINTS:

- Space between your words so your reader can read your writing. You have important things to say, so honor your ideas by leaving spaces between your words.
- Use end mark punctuation to tell your reader when to stop in your piece and how to read your sentences. It's important to take the time to reread your writing out loud and get help from a "Stop Spotter" if needed so you can put in end mark punctuation.

IN THIS TEXT:

Jacob spaces very nicely between his words.

WRITERS MIGHT CONSIDER:

Look at your writing RIGHT NOW! Are there spaces between your words? Show your writing to a partner. Does she agree with you?

IN THIS TEXT:

Jacob worked hard on his end mark punctuation:
- He approximates the use of exclamation marks when he excitedly states his opinion in the first line.
- He and his Stop Spotter (buddy) easily heard the stops in his writing and marked them with periods.

WRITERS MIGHT CONSIDER:

Look at your writing RIGHT NOW! Do you have periods, exclamations, or question marks, or is your writing one big long sentence? The best way to know where to put end marks is to read your writing out loud to yourself or someone else. When you hear the stops, put them in!

I like winter! I like winter because I have snowball fights. I like winter because I go sledding.

FOLLOW-UP TEACHING:

Spacing and end mark punctuation are issues across grade levels K–2.
Use the Cheerio trick. Repeat, repeat, repeat. Have Cheerios around for students to use as they need them. Assign students a Stop Spotter! This buddy listens to the author's writing, and says "STOP!" every time he hears a stop in the piece. (Often it's difficult for young writers to identify stops in their writing on their own.) Also, allow students to share their writing under the document camera so the whole class can help hear the stops and add punctuation. They love this, and everyone gains skill since you can model and guide. Continually celebrate spaces and end mark punctuation in everyday writing!

Opinion

FOCUS: Beginning opinions with signal phrases; supplying a reason for one's opinion

STANDARDS CONNECTION: Writing opinion pieces about topics; supplying a reason for an opinion; sharing with an audience

INSTRUCTIONAL CONTEXT: Students were learning about ways they could help in their communities. We read aloud a newspaper article about Jack, a second grade boy from our school who had opened his own snow cone stand to help earn money to care for a local police dog. Students were asked to write a letter to Jack, expressing their opinions about his actions. We delivered the letters to him, thus sharing our writing with an important audience.

TEACHING POINTS:

■ One way to begin an opinion piece is with a phrase like "In my opinion," so your purpose is clear right away.

■ Supply at least one reason for your opinion so others understand why you think the way you do.

IN THIS TEXT:

Emma begins with an opinion signal phrase:

I think that...

WRITERS MIGHT CONSIDER:

Brainstorm a list of other opinion signal phrases. Write the list on a poster so you can make additions and use the phrases when desired.

IN THIS TEXT:

Emma shares an explicit reason why she thinks Jack made a good decision.

I like your decision because you helped out your community.

WRITERS MIGHT CONSIDER:

Might Emma have elaborated more on her reason? I wonder, how did Jack's decision help the community?

She might have also thought about how the action may have made the dog or policemen feel.

I bet the policemen will be happy to use the money you earned to buy food and toys for the police dog!

To help you elaborate, think about how the subject of your opinion affects you. Jack's decision may affect Emma's future decisions in her community.

You inspired me to think about trying...

What opportunities might you have for writing opinions for real purposes and audiences?

For a reproducible version of this text, see page 125.

AUTHOR:
Emma
GRADE:
1

Dear Jack

I think that You made a good dashshin. I like your dasishin

because you helpt your community.
from Emma

Dear Jack,

I think that you made a good decision. I like your decision because you helped your community.

From,

Emma

FOLLOW-UP TEACHING:

Writing for real purposes is paramount in my classroom. When writers feel their thinking matters, their motivation soars, as does the quality of their work. Plus, they learn writing is REAL, not just for school. This is key to developing life-long writers. Start with the list below and try to frame several opinion pieces of writing around a real purpose.

- *To your librarian to acquire a new book you'd like in your school library*
- *To your teacher or principal about something at your school*
- *To a family member about your favorite family activity, asking to engage in it*
- *To a business about your opinion of a product or service*
- *To a community organization about your opinion of an event you attended*

Find easy ways to help your students share with stake-holding audiences. You'll often get responses which will send your writers over the moon!

Opinion

INSTRUCTIONAL CONTEXT: In my book *Stella Writes an Opinion*, Stella, a second-grade writer, is inspired to write an opinion about changing her school's policy so second graders can bring a morning snack, just like the kindergarten and first-grade students. Students were inspired to write their own opinion pieces about what they might change at our school after reading the book. After quickly revisiting the elements of an opinion, instruction focused on composing effective closings.

TEACHING POINTS:

- Closings should have a purpose. In this case, students are writing to influence behavior or policy, thus their closings should serve to inspire thought or action.
- The thinking, talking, and writing of our peers is powerful. It can push our own thinking to deeper levels or lead us to thoughts we may not have otherwise had. We can borrow phrases, examples, and language from other writers to use in our own writing.

IN THIS TEXT:

Colby crafts attention-grabbing language for his closing, hoping to inspire others to consider his cause:

Who's with me?

WRITERS MIGHT CONSIDER:

Play with other sentences, phrases, or questions that might inspire people to thought or action. What is another way Colby might have worded his ending to get a similar effect?

IN THIS TEXT:

Brenna, Colby's classmate, feels free to borrow Colby's language for her closing:

Who is with me?

WRITERS MIGHT CONSIDER:

What are some examples of wonderful language from your classmates: specific words, phrases, and sentences that were powerful or moved you? What do you think about the idea of "borrowing" them? Discuss this with your class. If you like this idea, you might keep a notebook of powerful peer examples you can refer to. Doing so helps all writers develop keen ears for the sounds of effective language.

AUTHOR:
Colby
GRADE:
1

I wihs we cane have saming elnfs then milk. becauss milk is gros. hos with me.

I wish we can have something else than milk because milk is gross. Who's with me?

AUTHOR:
Brenna
GRADE:
1

My opinion is that we should have more home work because then We lern who is with me?

My opinion is that we should have more homework because then we learn. Who is with me?

FOLLOW-UP TEACHING:

Search for other examples of call-to-action closings in texts you read. For example, I like to use book reviews from the Internet that were written by children. They often conclude with calls to action. Here's one: https://childtastic-books.wordpress.com/category/early-readersshort-chapter-books/ (Scroll down to Holly's review of the book. She ends her review with, "Find out by reading this book if you are interested in it.") Another source is the opinion or pro/con texts posted on www.newsela.com. Search "opinion" to find articles that may be appropriate to read aloud to your students (you can lower the lexile level), noting when you find call-to-action conclusions.

Keep a running list you can add to in a notebook or on a chart. When the class or an individual crafts an opinion meant to influence others, review the list to link to prior experience and ignite new thinking.

Opinion

★ **FOCUS:** Directly stating one's opinion; supplying explicit reasons for one's opinion

STANDARDS CONNECTION: Writing opinion pieces; naming the book; directly stating an opinion; supplying reasons for one's opinion

INSTRUCTIONAL CONTEXT: Students were given a choice of which books they would like to read next for literature circles (all readers in the small group read the same book and hold book club-like discussions as they proceed through the reading). They were asked to peruse the books, pick one they thought the group would enjoy, and state reasons for their choice, thus providing another authentic reason for opinion writing!

TEACHING POINTS:
- Alert your readers to the type of text you're writing and to your purpose by directly stating your opinion at the beginning of your piece.
- State reasons for your opinions. People want to know exactly why you feel the way you do. Reasons should be specific. The more you elaborate, the better others understand.

IN THIS TEXT:

Max directly names the book and then states his opinion in the first line:

> *I want to read* **Geronimo Stilton: Lost Treasure of the Emerald Eye..."**

Max uses capital letters to indicate the title.

The words

> *I want to read*

show Max's positive feeling about the book, indicating this is his choice for his literature circle group.

WRITERS MIGHT CONSIDER:

What are some additional ways Max could have stated his positive opinion? What alternative words might he have used to show he understood why he was writing his opinion? For example:

In my opinion, the group might enjoy...
The words *in my opinion* alert readers to what type of text they'll be reading.

My pick for our group is...
These words indicate an awareness of why the opinion is being written.

The book _____ is the best book for our group because...
These words indicate an awareness of why the opinion is being written.

IN THIS TEXT:

Max states specific reasons for his opinion and elaborates on each reason to help the reader understand.

> *...it's the first book of the series.*
This is his first reason for choosing this book.

> *...I like to read books in order.*
He provides additional detail as to why he wants to read the first book in the series.

> *I read on the back that they found a treasure map somewhere, and they want to find the treasure.*
This is his second reason. It is specific to the content of the book.

> *That sounds exciting.*
He elaborates on why the treasure map information is important to him.

WRITERS MIGHT CONSIDER:

I'd tell Max I'd like to know a bit more. Could he elaborate even further about the reasons behind his opinion by asking, *Why?* For example:

- *I like to read books in order.* (Why? I understand the characters or events more clearly. And/or... I can keep better track of what's happening if I read from the beginning to the end of a series.)

- *That sounds exciting.* (Why? It's always interesting to see what is in a lost treasure chest and/or treasure is often hidden in mysterious places. What a fun adventure it would be to go searching for it in unknown locations.)

AUTHOR:
Max

GRADE:
2

> I want to read Geronimo Stilton: Lost Treasure Of The Emerald Eye Because it's the First book of the series, And because I like to read books in order. Last, I read on the back that they found a treasure map somewhere, and they want to find the treasure. That sounds exciting!

I want to read *Geronimo Stilton: Lost Treasure of the Emerald Eye* because it's the first book of the series. And because I like to read books in order. Last, I read on the back that they found a treasure map somewhere, and they want to find the treasure. That sounds exciting!

FOLLOW-UP TEACHING:

Max did not provide a concluding statement or section in his opinion. This is understandable since this was an informal piece written for the purpose of voting on a book for his group. The standards ask writers to include a sense of closure beginning in first grade. When writing formally, this is an important element to teach, model, and find examples for students to emulate.

Naturally, when we offer students opportunities to express their opinions like this one, we show them the power they hold as writers by honoring them. In this case, sure enough, the book Max chose received the most votes so the group read it next.

Opinion

INSTRUCTIONAL CONTEXT: After hearing the book *Dog vs. Cat* by Chris Gall read aloud, students decided they enjoyed it so much, they wanted to write letters to our librarian to request she purchase a copy for our library. This authentic purpose for writing fit nicely into studying the elements of opinion writing since students realized they needed to tell the librarian *why* they thought she should purchase a copy. As we discussed this orally, many students said she should buy the book "because it is funny." The instructional focus became, "What makes the book funny?" What are specific examples, key details, or quotes you can share to prove how the book is funny so the librarian will be more apt to buy a copy?

TEACHING POINTS:

- Write opinions for real reasons.
- Elaborate on the reasons for your opinion by using specific information, examples, and key details—including quotes—directly from the text.

IN THIS TEXT:

Aiden recognizes the authentic reason for writing his opinion as he states in his first and last sentences:

- *I really hope you can get this book* **Dog vs. Cat** *by Chris Gall.*

- *Mrs. Harris, please get this book for the school.*

WRITERS MIGHT CONSIDER:

What are other authentic reasons for writing and sharing opinions? As students realize the importance of their opinions through your teaching, discussion, and use of mentor texts, they'll spot more opportunities to share their opinions. For example, if a student comes in after recess complaining about the lack of equipment, encourage him to write about it. List the idea on a Running Topics List (Wagstaff, 2011) to inspire others to look for real opportunities to share and write opinions. Adding to a Running Topics List on a regular basis can build students' abilities to recognize opportunities for opinion writing around topics that interest or concern them.

IN THIS TEXT:

Aiden uses specific examples from the text, including quotes, to explain why he thinks the book is funny and why the librarian should get a copy. His choices of quotes and examples are powerful, and he doesn't shy away from providing plenty of detail.

- *...at the end the cat said, 'What is that?' The dog pooped!"*

- *A baby moved in their room and they said, 'It stinks. Oh, the smell!' The creature never stops screeching."*

His choice of quotes is hilarious!

Also, their behavior was silly because they got each other in trouble like when the cat blows the dog whistle to make the dog howl, and the dog put catnip on the sofa and the cat tore all the sofa up!

This is a beautiful example of including all the detail necessary, both sides of the story, so to speak, to explain the crazy behavior of the characters.

WRITERS MIGHT CONSIDER:

Aiden uses two specific, funny quotes in his writing. What makes these quotes powerful? Might you consider using the actual words spoken by characters, the narrator of a story, or others (for example, quotes from people in a newspaper article) to support your points?

AUTHOR:
Aiden
GRADE:
2

Dear Mrs. Harris,

I really hope you can get this book Dog Vs. Cat by Chris Gall. One reason is because at the end the cat said, "What is that?" The dog pooped. A baby moved in their room and they said, "It stinks. Oh, the smell! The creature never stops screeching!" Then they decided to move out. Also, their behavior was silly because they got each other in trouble like when the cat blows the dog whistle to make the dog howl and the dog put catnip on the sofa and the cat tore all the sofa up! Mrs. Harris, please get this book for the school.

From,

Aiden

> Dear Mrs. Harris, I rely hope you can get this book Dog Vs. Cat by Chris Gall. One reson is because at the end the cat said "what is that?" the dog poopt. A baby moved in ther room and they said "it stinks, oh, the smell!

FOLLOW-UP TEACHING:

Work together as a class to collect powerful examples and quotes that support or illustrate a point. For example, if students say they like a book because it is funny, scary, or exciting, work with them to pull specific examples from the text (including quotes, when appropriate) that show *why* it is funny, scary, or exciting. Push students to go beyond typical responses like, "The book is funny because the characters do funny things." *What* did they do specifically? Encourage them to dig deeper. Model going back to the text repeatedly to reread and rethink. Make a record of your hard work by keeping examples in a notebook or recording them on a chart so they can be revisited. This helps make the thinking visible.

(When we write for real reasons, we have real audiences. In this case, the audience was our librarian. We delivered the letters to her. She not only bought copies of the book, she wrote each and every student a letter in response! You can't beat this for showing students the power of their voices and the importance of writing!)

Opinion

★ **FOCUS:** Using transitions and linking words throughout a piece

STANDARDS CONNECTION: Writing purposeful opinion pieces; using transitions and linking words to organize the piece

INSTRUCTIONAL CONTEXT: When students show emotion, capitalize on it. You'll often get their best writing because most will be oozing to get their feelings out. John was very upset about how The Hundreds Club was being handled at the school, so he decided to write to the principal to see if the policy could be changed.

TEACHING POINTS:
- ■ Use transitions in your writing to connect ideas, improve sentence flow, and guide your readers from one thought to the next or one section to the next.
- ■ Use linking words to connect your opinion with your reasons.

IN THIS TEXT:

John uses several different types of transitions:

> ***Here's why.***

This sentence connects John's opinion to his reasons. It's a good alternative to linking the two with the word *because*.

> ***A few months ago, …***

John is ready to tell about the personal experience that led to the formation of his opinion.

> ***But, since it was close to the end of the month, …***

The word *but* signals the reader that John will include details about the problem next.

> ***This way,…***

John has presented what he thinks is a solution to the problem. The phrase *this way* signals he's about to tell why he thinks his idea could be a solution. It connects one sentence to another, or one idea to the next idea.

WRITERS MIGHT CONSIDER:

Borrow some of John's transitions and try them out loud. For example, state your opinion about which candy bar you like the best. Then say, *Here's why,* and follow that up with your reasons.

Try another. State your opinion about a school issue. Like, *"I think we should get two recycling bins, one for paper and one for plastic."*

Now, try John's phrase, *This way…* to signal you'll be sharing why you think this.

IN THIS TEXT:

John uses a more common linking word to connect his opinion to his reasons:

> ***I think it would be better to leave the posters up all year <u>since</u> kids work so hard…***

WRITERS MIGHT CONSIDER:

Typical linking words for opinion writing are *because*, *and*, *also*, and *but*. Find a spot or two where any of these would fit in John's piece. Evaluate which version of his writing is better. Why?

AUTHOR:
John

GRADE:
2

Dear Mr. Stevenson,

This is John Dorius. I am writing to you with my opinion. I think that we should leave the 100s club posters up in the hall all year. Here's why. A few months ago, I made the 100s club finally after waiting a very long time. It was around the end of the month. I was so excited to have my name on that poster. I brought my grandma in to show her that I'd finally made the club.

But, since it was so close to the end of the month, the poster was only up a few days. I went to look at it again, and my name was gone. I felt bad and sad. I think it would be better to leave the posters up all year since kids work so hard to get to be part of the club. This way, they can feel proud and be happy about their accomplishment all year long.

Sincerely,

John Dorius

FOLLOW-UP TEACHING:

Incorporating the types of transitions John used here is more difficult than using simple transition words. Collecting a list of common words and phrases and categorizing them by purpose is helpful, especially if you model using them while you're writing. Highlight them in your pieces and discuss what purpose they serve as you use them. This will create a foundation for students to build upon as they grow. Celebrate those who experiment with these phrases in their writing and share them under the document camera.

One day me
went to lago
the roller
went on X car
took for like
get on the r
huge
of the ^ line
I got on
me and my
the waits
in a tank ^ t

Student Mentor Texts
NARRATIVE

Personal Narrative

INSTRUCTIONAL CONTEXT: Sometimes students burst into the classroom with stories spilling from their lips. Take advantage of these times by inviting them to share their stories aloud. Excitement will undoubtedly flood the room. Share your own personal story, model some writing, and invite students to write. My picture book, *Stella Tells Her Story*, demonstrates how you might happily see this process through all the way to sharing with an audience.

TEACHING POINTS:

- Get your writing down on paper the best you can. Drawing is a great way to communicate your story, record it, and help you remember the story you want to tell so you can share it.
- Add labels to your drawing(s). Listen to the sounds you hear in the words and put down some matching letters to identify who or what is in your picture(s).

IN THIS TEXT:

Felix gets his writing down the best he can. He really wants to tell his story, and we want to hear it! He uses drawing to tell his story.

- Notice his story has two characters. Given the detail Felix has included, you can tell one is probably older than the other.

- You can see the characters are angry. See the frown on the shorter one's face (that's Felix) and the frown and angry eye on the taller one's face (that's Felix's sister). Also notice the sphere with swirls above Felix's head. This indicates his angry feelings, too.

WRITERS MIGHT CONSIDER:

Since Felix is telling his story about a time he and his sister had a disagreement, what else would you like to see in the picture? What details might he also have included? Why?

- For example, I'm wondering what he and his sister are disagreeing about (his sister had taken his favorite toy). Could that be included somehow?

- I'd love to know more. What did his sister do with the toy? Did he get it back? Perhaps Felix could have included another picture to tell more of the story.

IN THIS TEXT:

Felix labels the two characters in his story. This helps the reader get more meaning and helps Felix better remember his story so he can share it.

The shorter character is labeled with the letter *m* for *me*.

The taller character is labeled with the letter *s* for *sister*.

Felix was able to hear the beginning sounds in each of these words and match them with the correct letter (using a Word Wall).

WRITERS MIGHT CONSIDER:

What other sounds do you hear in the words Felix labeled? Could you include more letters in your labels?

In terms of phonemic awareness and writing development, if children can indicate beginning sounds, they may be able to hear and indicate ending sounds. So, for example, they may say they could label *s-r* for *sister*.

What, besides the characters, might Felix have labeled? He might have labeled the angry, swirly ball he included with *m* for *mad* or *f* for *feelings*.

Have you ever listened for sounds in words and labeled your pictures with the letters that match, as best you can? How will this help you? (This helps you grow as a writer and speller because you are working to use what you are learning about words, letters, and sounds. It gives you another clue to help you remember your story and helps others reread your story.)

AUTHOR:
Felix
GRADE:
K

FOLLOW-UP TEACHING:

Model writing your own personal narrative through drawing and labeling.
This can be done small group if most of your students are beyond this stage
or, if not, model this approach several times in front of the whole group.
Be sure to demonstrate how you listen inside words for sounds and identify letters
to record (making connections to your Word Wall or other resources). You can
model on plain white paper, and your story could span several pages to include
several details. As always, celebrate students' drawing and labeling under the
document camera to encourage them to use what they know and keep growing!

Personal Narrative

★ **FOCUS:** Writing a personal story focused on a single event, including the setting, who was there, and what happened

STANDARDS CONNECTION: Using a combination of drawing and writing to narrate a single event

INSTRUCTIONAL CONTEXT: Every primary grade teacher knows young children enjoy sharing personal stories! Our kindergarten teachers have their students write personal narratives about their families at least three times a year. They examine these samples as one way to determine students' writing growth and needs. Molly wrote the following story during one of these periods. Preceding the writing, we read *Black is Brown is Tan* by Arnold Adoff, a poem about families that is beautifully portrayed in a picture book.

TEACHING POINTS:

■ Write a story about a single event you've experienced.

■ Include the setting, who was there, and what you did. Show these elements with your words and your illustration(s).

IN THIS TEXT:

Molly keeps her story focused on a single event.

- Her whole piece is about her trip to the beach with her family and what they did there.

- She does not veer off into other events or other stories.

WRITERS MIGHT CONSIDER:

What are some experiences you have had with family members? Make a list. Who was involved in each event? What was the event? Be sure to focus on just one event, one time, one happening. You can use your list for ideas for future story writing.

IN THIS TEXT:

Molly includes the setting, who was there, and some details about what happened. She does this with both her words and her picture.

I went to the beach…
Notice the beach shown in the picture. We can see the water, the waves, and the sand. Those are great details that took some effort.

…with mom and my dad and grandparents…
Notice how Molly not only named her characters in her words, but also included them in her picture, even labeling them to make her story more clear for the reader.

On the last line she also includes that they brought their dog.
This is indicated in her picture as well.

…to collect seashells and decorate sand castles…
This part tells us what Molly and her family did at the beach. Notice the related details in Molly's picture: her family members carry pails to collect seashells.

WRITERS MIGHT CONSIDER:

What do you like, or not like, about Molly's story? What questions would you still ask her about her trip to the beach? What else might she have included? How does her illustration help us understand or build interest in the story?

AUTHOR:
Molly
GRADE:
K

I went to the beach with mom and my dad and grandparents to collect seashells and decorate sand castles...
(indiscernible) and dog.

FOLLOW-UP TEACHING:

To stimulate personal narrative writing, I often ask students to think of a time when they were happy, sad, excited, scared, or angry. I ask who they were with and what happened. This helps them focus on a single event. We share and have them talk-out their stories before writing. As suggested in the first Writers Might Consider, the list of events and people students create will make great fodder for discussion, oral storytelling, and writing.

Fictional Narrative

★ **FOCUS:** Including fictional happenings

STANDARDS CONNECTION: Writing fictional narratives

INSTRUCTIONAL CONTEXT: The class practiced building fictional stories together by telling "add-on" stories aloud. The teacher would begin a story, setting the scene and bringing in characters, relating this to the narrative text structure students had learned and studied in their reading. Then, students would volunteer to add to the story. Naturally, the class enjoyed numerous stories read aloud to prepare them for writing their own fictional narratives.

TEACHING POINTS:

■ Include a character or characters in your story.

■ This is a made-up story. Include some fictional happenings like we do when we tell our "add-on" stories. What will your character(s) do?

IN THIS TEXT:

Violet includes just one character (herself):

> *One day I was a...*

WRITERS MIGHT CONSIDER:

Fictional stories can include all kinds of characters: people, animals, superheroes, villains, ...

What kind of characters would you like to include in a fictional narrative? Why?

IN THIS TEXT:

Violet realizes this is a made-up story, including many fictional happenings:

- *One day I was a snowman, then I turned into a mermaid. I liked it. I loved it!*

- *Then I flew. I flew up, up, up, up to the sun.*

WRITERS MIGHT CONSIDER:

Imagine becoming something other than yourself. What would you be? Why? Write about what you would do by following Violet's lead:
One day, I was a... then I turned into a ...

If you were writing this story, what would happen next? Reread the last sentence. Does it feel like the end? What does this mean for your story writing?

AUTHOR:
Violet

GRADE:
K

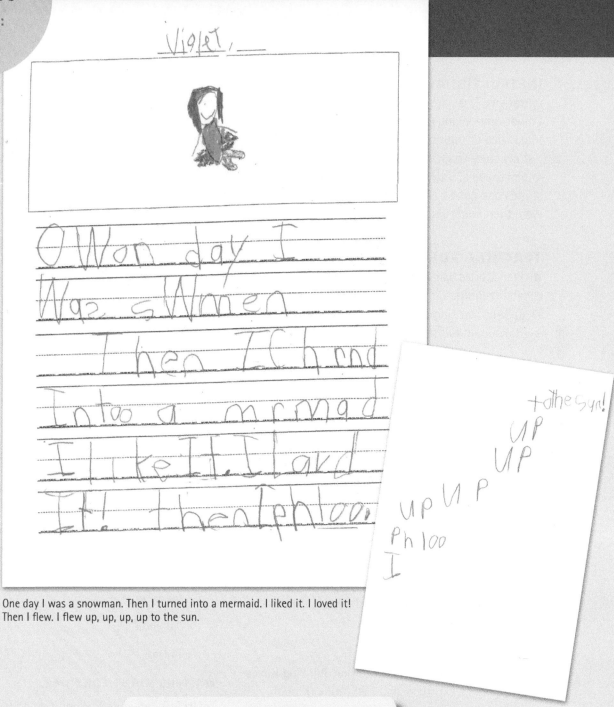

One day I was a snowman. Then I turned into a mermaid. I liked it. I loved it!
Then I flew. I flew up, up, up, up to the sun.

FOLLOW-UP TEACHING:

Try telling a story orally using the add-on technique. If you show loads of
enthusiasm and play with words and events as you add to the story, students
will as well. They'll be ready to have a ball imagining and writing their very own
fictional stories in no time!

Personal Narrative

★ **FOCUS:** Planning and orally rehearsing a personal narrative; including relevant details and craft elements

STANDARDS CONNECTION: Writing personal narratives, including details to describe actions, thoughts, and feelings

INSTRUCTIONAL CONTEXT: Students used Thinking Boxes (Wagstaff, 2011, 2016) to plan personal narratives. They labeled their boxes with temporal words as a support to help them think through events. I modeled thinking aloud and recording notes and sketches in one box at a time, after which the students filled each of their boxes, one at a time. When the last box was filled in, I went back and modeled talking-out my story again, this time adding details for actions, thoughts, and feelings using speech bubbles and onomatopoeia. Students did the same. As they prepared to write, they partnered up and talked-out their stories one more time to make sure they were complete. Buoyed by their repeated oral rehearsals, they were then ready and eager to write, using the graphic organizer as a guide.

TEACHING POINTS:

■ Plan stories using a graphic organizer (Thinking Boxes); add details to describe actions, thoughts, and feelings.

■ Talk-out writing as it develops (Wagstaff, 2016). This often leads to making additions. Then, rehearse it again, in full sentences, before you write and as you write.

IN THIS TEXT:

Ruby plans her story from beginning to end. She includes notes and sketches in each box about what occurs when she goes to gymnastics; then she goes back and adds speech bubbles. For example:

> *My teacher helps me do handstands*

Her words and sketch help her remember to include the people involved in her story. Her speech bubble reminds her of what her teacher says as she helps her.

> *Love it*

She added these words to remind herself of how she feels at that moment.

WRITERS MIGHT CONSIDER:

Try it! Plan a personal narrative using Thinking Boxes labeled First, Next, Then, and Last. Think through what happened in the order that events occurred. Jot notes and sentences and make sketches to remind yourself of what you'll write when you record your story on paper.

IN THIS TEXT:

Ruby talked-out her story in full sentences several times before she wrote. This helped her pinpoint just how she wanted to word it on paper. It also prompted her to make additions to her Thinking Boxes:

> *She helps me do a cartwheel.*

When Ruby talked this out, she said,

> *Cartwheels are my favorite, and I'm really good at them!*

Then, she added these notes:

- *favorite*
- *I'm good*
- *Ta Da!*

WRITERS MIGHT CONSIDER:

Try it! Talk-out your writing using a graphic organizer. As you talk, make whole sentences, changing words as you go to get things just the way you want them. Think. As you talk, do you find you are including more details than what was initially in your Thinking Boxes? Add notes, details to sketches, speech bubbles, etc. Talk-it-out to a partner again before you write. Do you think this process made your story better?

There is more about Talking-It-Out on page 98.

AUTHOR:
Ruby
GRADE:
1

1st Thinking Box: (First) I went to gymnastics on Tuesday.

2nd Thinking Box (Next) My teacher helps me do handstands.   Good job. Love it.

3rd Thinking box (Then) She helps me do a cartwheel. favorite   ta da! I'm good

4th Thinking Box (Last) Our parents watch us. I love it!

FOLLOW-UP TEACHING:

Thinking Boxes are a useful tool for planning informative and opinion writing, as well. For informative writing, students can list their topic in the first box; then, as they talk-it-out, fill in words for an introduction. In the second and third boxes they can include notes and sketches about main ideas (or questions) and details (or answers). In the fourth box they might plan how they will conclude their piece.

For an opinion piece, students record their opinion in the first box, reasons and details in boxes two and three, and their concluding idea in the last box. Change the number of boxes to differentiate for your students' needs. Also, don't forget to model and have them talk-it-out as they plan and write. Oral language is a scaffold for writers that is often underutilized. You'll see a huge difference in students' writing if you take advantage of this strategy!

Personal Narrative

★ **FOCUS:** Word choice; writing long

STANDARDS CONNECTION: Writing personal narratives; attending to word choice

INSTRUCTIONAL CONTEXT: Rather than modeling, I used peer mentor texts (both Thinking Boxes and stories) to focus and engage students in planning and writing their own narratives. Students used the process Ruby and her class followed to plan their stories using temporal words in Thinking Boxes (see page 58). Then while writing, we conferred about and stopped to celebrate their word choice. Additionally, we looked for places to linger, to tell more and write long, meaning to purposefully focus on a point or moment in time in order to write as much as possible about it.

TEACHING POINTS:
- Focus on your word choice. Choose juicy, precise, unusual words to show your exact meaning and add interest to your writing.
- Write long. Find places in your writing where you can linger, stay in the moment and include as many details as possible.

IN THIS TEXT:

Tayvin carefully considered his word choice:

- *It took like forever to get on the ride...*
- *because of the huge line.*
- *When we got to the top it went crazy fast...*
- *...I wanted to go 50 times more!*

WRITERS MIGHT CONSIDER:

Try it! Reread a piece of your writing. Find a spot where you've used an ordinary word and substitute a more descriptive or exciting word choice. Find a spot where you can add an effective word or phrase. Share your changes with a peer. How does your writing sound now?

IN THIS TEXT:

Tayvin tried to stretch his writing, lingering to reflect on a moment and write longer:

> *First, me and my dad went in a tunnel.*

When Tayvin reread, and attempted to stay longer in this moment, he added,

> *The wall were bull heads.*

WRITERS MIGHT CONSIDER:

I would ask Tayvin to stay even longer in the tunnel. Was it dark? How was he feeling while he was there? What else did he see?

There are other places where Tayvin may have lingered to write longer in this piece. Can you find some?

For a reproducible version of this text, see pages 138–139.

★

AUTHOR:
Tayvin

GRADE:
1

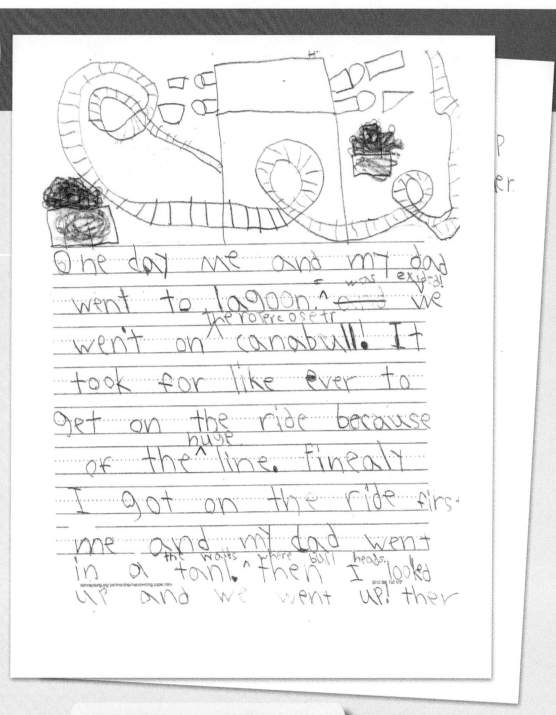

One day me and my dad
went to Lagoon. I was
excited! We went on the
rollercoaster Cannibal. It
took for like ever to get
on the ride because of the
huge line. Finally, I got on
the ride. First, me and my
dad went in a tunnel. The
walls were bullheads. Then,
I looked up and we went up!
Then, when we got to the
top, it went crazy fast then
the ride was over! I got off
and I wanted to go 50 times
more!

FOLLOW-UP TEACHING:

Word choice is a constant focus as we "read like writers." Again, I suggest
keeping a class notebook to record noteworthy examples of effective word choice.
Reflect on how word choice improves a piece and celebrate students' examples!

"Writing long" is a strategy you can reinforce all year. Give students a small
moment like, "Pretend you're picking an apple off a tree. Close your eyes and
visualize. Where are you? How are you picking the apple? What do you do? What
do you see, smell, hear? Now, write just about that moment, linger there, write
long, don't evaluate, just write as much as you can." When you share examples,
talk about what lingering in a moment and writing long can do for a piece of
writing. Then, help students pinpoint opportunities for writing long on their own.

Narrative

★ **FOCUS:** Revising; changing content to add more detail and answer questions asked by others

STANDARDS CONNECTION: Focusing on a topic; responding to questions and suggestions from peers; adding details to strengthen writing as needed

INSTRUCTIONAL CONTEXT: The reading of several narratives in the students' core reading program led to the writing of personal narratives. We created an anchor chart to include the essential elements along with possible craft elements writers might use. We brainstormed topics, planned our stories, and I modeled writing my own narrative, adding to it day by day while consulting the chart. The class followed suit. As students wrote, we shared their ongoing pieces with each other, asking questions to inspire revision.

TEACHING POINTS:

■ Revise to make changes to clarify your content, paint a clearer picture, or answer questions asked.
■ Once a revision is made, reread to make sure the piece still makes sense. If you've added a lot, make sure the placement works.

IN THIS TEXT:

Caden made several revisions to his story to clarify his content based on questions asked by me and his peers. Here are some notable instances:

Caden had written,

> *But after it was fun.*

I asked, "After what?" He added,

> *we got in the air it was fun.*

Caden's next sentence read:

> *We went on a boat to the Bahamas.*

A peer was confused because Caden had just been talking about the plane. He added to the sentence,

> *When we got off the airplane, we went on a boat to the Bahamas.*

When asked why he didn't like the boat ride, he added two sentences:

> *I did not feel good. I felt like I could barf.*

Though not eloquent, this did the job of clarifying and connected logically to the next sentence,

> *My friend got sick like me.*

WRITERS MIGHT CONSIDER:

Caden made nine revisions to his story, all of which came about because someone asked him questions as he read his piece. Read his story once without the revisions. Now read it again with the revisions. Which version is better? Why?

IN THIS TEXT:

In response to another question, Caden added three sentences to the end of his piece. Upon rereading, he recognized this new chunk of text did not fit at the end. He had to reread to identify where it would fit, and he drew an arrow to indicate its placement.

Caden initially ended his piece with the sentence:

> *My favorite part of the trip was when I swam in the ocean.*

I asked him why this was his favorite part. He described what he saw as he swam:

> *I saw coral and fish. I liked the green coral and fish. They were pretty blue.*

When he reread the story including these new sentences, he realized it didn't feel like the end anymore. I asked him where the new sentences might fit instead. He experimented by rereading from the spot where the arrow is now pointing. After rereading, he was satisfied that the new sentences did indeed fit there, so he drew the arrow.

WRITERS MIGHT CONSIDER:

Consider how important it is to listen carefully when a writer shares his work with you, and to ask questions when you have them. You can help your peers make their writing so much better! By asking questions and making revisions, you become a better writer, too!

AUTHOR:
Caden
GRADE:
2

> caden
> One morning, I went to the
> When i woke up
> airport. When I got to the
> With my friends. becuase it was my first time
> airport I was exited. But When
> I got on the airplane. I felt
> to florida When we got off
> the airplane
> sick. But after it was fun. We
> we got in the air it was fun.
> went on a boat to the bhahamas.
> I did not like the boat ride. My
> were prety

One morning, when I woke up, I went to the airport with my friends. When I got to the airport, I was excited because it was my first time. But, when I got on the airplane to Florida, I felt sick. But, after we got in the air, it was fun. When we got off the airplane, we went on a boat ride to the Bahamas. I did not like the boat ride. I did not feel good. I felt like I could barf. My friend got sick like me. When we got to the Bahamas, I swam in the ocean. I saw coral and fish. I liked the green coral and fish. They were pretty blue. It was fun. My favorite part of the trip was when I swam in the ocean.

FOLLOW-UP TEACHING:

The Just Ask It strategy (Wagstaff, 2011, 2016) is an easy way to help students make revisions to their writing. Students simply pair up to listen to one another's pieces. If a question pops into a listener's head, he just asks it, causing the writer to consider revision. By engaging in this practice regularly, we hope students internalize the importance of reading and rereading while they write. This will help them identify places where questions might be asked, and where clarification or additions might be needed. Make this practice a part of your weekly schedule, allowing children to pair up frequently as they produce a piece over time. To start, teach them to ask simple Who, What, When, Where, Why, and How questions. Additionally, modeled writing is key. As you model, be sure to think aloud about revision, rereading, crossing out, making additions, clarifying, moving chunks of text, or reworking an ending or beginning. When students see and hear you do this, you will see them apply revision techniques in their own writing.

Personal Narrative

★ **FOCUS:** Focusing on one small moment within a series of events, using descriptive details

STANDARDS CONNECTION: Writing personal narratives, including details to describe actions, thoughts, and feelings

INSTRUCTIONAL CONTEXT: Personal narratives are treasures. Writing and sharing them builds classroom community while bolstering students' own identities. I modeled and students followed as we planned our stories around small moments (Oxenhorn and Calkins, 2003) using Thinking Boxes (see Ruby's example on page 56), talked-them-out, and added details that focused on our thoughts and feelings during the events.

TEACHING POINTS:

■ Focus on writing about a small moment within a larger event. By focusing small, you have to notice and include particular details. This also helps you avoid simply listing a bunch of stuff that happened.

■ Add details that focus on your thoughts and feelings about events to let readers inside your head to experience your stories in a deeper way.

IN THIS TEXT:

Gabe focuses on a small moment, the catching of fish, rather than a play-by-play of his entire camping trip with his dad.

- His story has a focus. We know what moment within the three-day trip had the most meaning for Gabe.

- Because Gabe is focused on this small moment, he includes relevant details:

  - *We were going fishing very close to the water.*

  - *We waited a long time to get a fish.*

  - *Finally, we got a little fish.*

  - *We cut the skin off so another fish would eat the skin.*

  - *Then we caught a big fish.*

WRITERS MIGHT CONSIDER:

What are some events you'd like to write about? Within these bigger events, identify the most important moments. What part of the story could you laser focus in on so you don't just list a bunch of stuff you did?

IN THIS TEXT:

Since we planned the outline of our stories in our Thinking Boxes, then went back to consider our reactions to the small moments along the way in our stories by adding notes to our boxes, Gabe was able to easily incorporate these details into his text:

- *It was so boring. It seemed like forever!*

- *Finally, we got a little fish. Woo hoo!*

- *And we cooked it and ate it. Ick! I don't like the taste of fish, but it was still fun!*

WRITERS MIGHT CONSIDER:

Look back at a story you've written. Reread it, listening for places where you can add reactions using words for your thoughts and feelings. How were you feeling at different points in your story? How does adding these details make your story better?

See the Follow-up Teaching points accompanying Molly's piece, page 55, for ideas to help students brainstorm topics.

For a reproducible version of this text, see page 142.

AUTHOR:
Gabe
GRADE:
2

ent camping in the mountains with my dad. We were going fishing very clos to the watr. We wated a long time to get a fish. It was so boring! It Seemed like forever! Finaly we gote a littl fish. Woo hoo! We cut the scin off so anather fish wold eat the Scin. Then we cot a big fish. And we ckooct it and ate it. Ick! I downt like the tast of fish but it was Still fun!

I went camping in the mountains with my dad. We were going fishing very close to the water. We waited a long time to get a fish. It was so boring! It seemed like forever! Finally, we caught a little fish. Woo hoo! We cut the skin off so another fish would eat the skin. Then, we caught a big fish. And we cooked it and ate it. Ick! I don't like the taste of fish but it was still fun!

FOLLOW-UP TEACHING:

Watch how writers incorporate details for actions, thoughts, and feelings in their trade books. Reread these parts. Read them with and without these details so students hear the difference. Record particularly noteworthy examples in a class notebook for future reference.

Fictional Narrative

★ **FOCUS:** Understanding that stories need a beginning, middle, and end; using dialogue to bring stories to life

STANDARDS CONNECTION: Writing fictional narratives; adding the element of dialogue

INSTRUCTIONAL CONTEXT: As we prepared to write fictional narratives, we went back to familiar mentor texts like *Where The Wild Things Are* (Sendak) and *If I Built a Car* (Van Dusen). We talked about ideas, listed several, and excitedly played with details aloud. (For example, "Your spaceman could say, "Golly bazooka! I'm going to crash land on Mars!") We sketched out our beginnings, middles, and ends, and then we wrote. As students wrote, I encouraged them to add dialogue to their pieces, modeling by adding this element to my own.

TEACHING POINTS:
■ Use your imagination and the fictional narratives we've read as models to write a fictional story complete with beginning, middle, and end.
■ Add dialogue to your story to make characters come to life and add an interesting element to your work.

IN THIS TEXT:

Daysen uses his imagination, writing a story about Legos coming to life. His story has a beginning, middle, and end.

Notice how Daysen has a *B* at the top of the page to signify his beginning, an *M* for the middle, and an *E* for the end.

> *I was building with my Legos when Mom came in and said, 'Time for bed!' I went to bed. When Mom was asleep, I heard something. Eeck! My door opened. I got a little scared.*

Daysen begins by setting the scene for the story and building suspense.

> *When I saw my Legos walking across my door. I whispered, "Wow, this is epic..." Suddenly, my Legos spotted me! I hid under my covers...*

The middle of Daysen's story is all about becoming friends with the Legos.

> *We watched Goosebumps, Star Wars, and scary movies. We played video games. It was epic. Every night, the Legos would come to life.*

At the end of his story, Daysen tells what he and the Legos did together. After prompting and answering questions posed by his classmates, he added that they would come to life every night.

WRITERS MIGHT CONSIDER:

Fictional narratives might begin with setting the scene, action, or talk (among others). Which technique does Daysen use? Try out a different beginning.

IN THIS TEXT:

Daysen uses dialogue to bring the middle of his story to life! (I conferenced with him to help him place the quotation marks.)

> *"You don't have to be scared," said Lego Emit.*

This was a great way to move the action forward since the narrator was hiding under the covers.

> *"I don't?" I said.*
> *"You don't."*
> *"We are all friends," said Lego Batman.*

Since the narrator was scared, we were wondering if the Legos were friends or foes. The dialogue between characters answers this.

> *"Yeah. We can stay up late."*
> *"Ha! We can!" said the Lego.*
> *"Awesome!" I said. "This is gonna' be great."*

The characters are clearly building their camaraderie as shown in the dialogue. The talk sounds real.

WRITERS MIGHT CONSIDER:

When using dialogue, we can add some variety to our word choice by using different words for *said*. Read Daysen's dialogue again. Substitute other words for *said*. How does it sound now?

AUTHOR:
Daysen
GRADE:
2

Daysen
The night the legos came
to life
I was buliding with my legos
when mom came in and said
"Time for bed!" I went to bed.
when mom was asleep I
herd something. eeck! my
dor opend. I got a littel
scared. when I saw my legos
walking acrost my door!
I wisperd "wow this is^epic.

The Night The Legos Came to Life

I was building with my Legos when mom came in and said, "Time for bed!" I went to bed. When mom was asleep, I heard something. Eeck! My door opened. I got a little scared. When I saw my Legos walking across my door! I whispered, "Wow, this is epic." Suddenly, my Legos spotted me! I hid under my covers. "You don't have to be scared," said Lego Emmet.

"I don't?" I said.

"You don't."

"We are all friends," said Lego Batman.

"Cool!" I said. "Yay! We can stay up late."

"Ha! We can!" said the Lego.

"Awesome," I said. "This is gonna' be great!" I said.

We watched Goosebumps, Star Wars, and scary movies. We played video games. It was epic. Every night, the Legos would come to life.

FOLLOW-UP TEACHING:

Create even more excitement by having students pick someone to share their fictional stories with outside of the classroom. I use a response card. I have them fill in the blanks to encourage the person they share with to write a response back. A reproducible example is on page 155.

Emma

this morning
wen I was
I chript ar
sistr helpt
up.

Student Mentor Texts
OTHER TEXT TYPES

Poetry

INSTRUCTIONAL CONTEXT: After reading the sections about poetry walks in my book *Stella: Poet Extraordinaire*, the students and I grabbed blank paper and clipboards and went outside for a spring walk. We jotted down words and phrases for anything 'springish' that caught our attention. We also quickly sketched to capture our thinking. When we came in, I modeled writing a free verse line based on one of my jottings. I then invited students to take just one of their jottings and turn it into a line or phrase, following my model. We continued this process until we had at least four lines with which to create our spring poems.

TEACHING POINTS:

- Know what to do during a poetry walk. Use this quiet time to make observations about the topic. Freely jot words and phrases, and sketch on your paper.
- Turn your jottings into a poem.

IN THIS TEXT:

Brennan made several quick sketches and labeled them during our poetry walk.

He sketched some flowers growing and labeled them
> *flawrs.*

He sketched some clouds, labeling them
> *white clowds.*

He sketched a branch with some tiny leaves, labeling these
> *leevs.*

WRITERS MIGHT CONSIDER:

How might sketching, labeling, and quickly jotting words and phrases lead to other writing? How is this process helpful to writers? When could you use it?

IN THIS TEXT:

Brennan followed my model, using four of his sketches (though he had more) to create his lines. He also added a final line, which I love:

- *Leaves on trees.*
- *Wind is blowing.*
- *Flowers blooming.*
- *Rain drops!*
- *Here's spring!*

WRITERS MIGHT CONSIDER:

Enjoy a poetry walk right now! You might be surprised at how you can turn simple jottings and sketches into something magical!

**AUTHOR:
Brennan**

**GRADE:
K**

Leevs on trees.
Wind is blowing.
flawrs blowming.
rone drops.
hers spring!

Leaves on trees.
Wind is blowing.
Flowers blooming.
Rain drops.
Here's spring!

FOLLOW-UP TEACHING:

Provide students with guided experiences in turning words into phrases to support their abilities to write poetry. Give them an ordinary, everyday word such as *milk* and have them create a meaningful phrase. Ask, *"Milk...what? Milk... where? Milk...when?,"* etc. Students love sharing their phrases, and before you know it, you'll have them hooked on this kind of language play. This is also a good context for working on parts of speech.

Honor students' poetry writing by typing the poems, having students illustrate them, and binding them together in a class book. Students love to check the book out of the classroom library to take home to share.

List

★ **FOCUS:** Brainstorming writing topics

STANDARDS CONNECTION: Creating a habit of generating one's own writing topics; stretching students' writing repertoires into varied genres

INSTRUCTIONAL CONTEXT: Many teachers have their students keep Topics Lists. I scaffold my writers by maintaining an ongoing *class* Running Topics List (Wagstaff, 2011) on our main whiteboard. When writing ideas come up (in class, on the playground, based on talk by the coat rack, etc.), we briefly chat about them and add them to our Running List. This way, students see an important habit of mind modeled, and they learn what these lists are really about. They are invited to keep their own lists and add to them at any time, including recording topics from our class list that they think may interest them.

TEACHING POINTS:

■ Writers are always looking and listening for ideas. We write down our ideas so they are not lost.

■ Writers stretch themselves. They try different writing genres, even in their own choice writing (i.e., beyond class assignments).

IN THIS TEXT:

Cynesha clearly understands the purpose of a Topics List and adds to it dutifully based on her own experiences. I know she is looking and listening for ideas and taking the time to record them as good writers do. She also checks off topics she's already written about.

She has eight topics on her list so far:

Best Pet
Grandma Cookies Making
Letter to Ashlee
Chameleons! Info Book
Favorite Sport—gymnastics
RULES! for Game
Book Poster READ Click Clack Moo
Crayons Poem

She has checked off three of her topics because she has already written these pieces.

WRITERS MIGHT CONSIDER:

What is the value of keeping a Topics List? Where will you keep yours? When will you add to the list? Do you think checking off ideas you've written about is a good idea? Why? When you add a topic to your list does this mean you *have to* write about it?

IN THIS TEXT:

Cynesha stretches herself as a writer. She records ideas based on multiple genres and is exploring them in her choice writing.

Best Pet
She wrote an opinion piece about how a dog makes the best pet. She checked this off her list.

Grandma Cookies Making
She's considering writing a personal narrative about an experience with her grandma.

Letter to Ashlee
She wrote an informal, friendly letter to a classmate.

Chameleons! Info Book
She's considering writing an informational piece about chameleons and publishing it in book format.

Favorite Sport—gymnastics
She's thinking about writing another opinion piece about her favorite sport.

RULES! for game
She wrote a list of rules and a step-by-step how-to piece on a game she made up at recess. She wanted to make sure her playmates were clear about the rules and how to play the game.

WRITERS MIGHT CONSIDER:

Do you stretch yourself as a writer? Do you try different writing types? Take out your list and color code your topics into categories. If you don't see a lot of color variety, where might you stretch more?

AUTHOR:
Cynesha
GRADE:
1

best pet ✓
grama cookces making

letr to Ashlee ✓
kamluns! info book

favret sport—jimnastks

RuLES! for game ✓

book Postr READ Click clack moo
crains Poem

Best pet
Grandma cookies making
Letter to Ashlee
Chameleons! Info book
Favorite sport-gymnastics
RULES! for game
Book poster READ Click Clack Moo
Crayons Poem

FOLLOW-UP TEACHING:

We have a balance between choice writing and assigned writing. Teachers have standards to teach and specific genres to cover, so we do this in workshop through different tasks and assignments. But, writers also have to develop the ability to come up with and write about their own topics. They are highly motivated by choice, and this brings a lot of joy (and surprise!) to the writing classroom.

Keep a class Running Topics List all year so the habit of listening and looking for writing ideas is continually practiced. Also, when you see students interacting with their lists, celebrate them! Put their lists under the document camera and share. When they've written a piece that was on their list, share it! This will keep the momentum going.

About the Author Page

INSTRUCTIONAL CONTEXT: Students so enjoyed writing and sharing fictional narratives that we decided to publish them in book form to put in our classroom library for check-out. To make the experience even more relevant, we had students create covers and About the Author pages. (For additional excitement, we printed Reader Comments on the back of this page to encourage written responses to one another's work. They loved it!)

TEACHING POINTS:
- ▪ Understand the structure and purpose of an About the Author page.
- ▪ Include only relevant information in an About the Author page.

IN THIS TEXT:

Cambry understands that the purpose of the About the Author page is to introduce herself to her readers. She understands the structure as well, using third person:

- She begins with her full name as an introduction. (It is blacked-out here for privacy.)

- She uses the third person pronoun *she* throughout the piece.

WRITERS MIGHT CONSIDER:

Study different About the Author sections in books and online. What are the structures you see?

IN THIS TEXT:

Cambry includes only relevant personal information on her About the Author page:

- *Cambry likes her family and the colors pink and purple and blue and black.*

- *She really likes her dad and her mom, not really her brothers...*

- *...and her friends are Gracie and Lizzy.*

WRITERS MIGHT CONSIDER:

What other information might Cambry have included on her About the Author page? I might ask her why she wrote the story, or where her idea came from. Authors often include this kind of information in their About the Author pages. What kind of information would not be appropriate? Why?

Create your own About the Author page to include at the end of books you publish. You can bring in a photo to use, get one from your teacher, or draw a small portrait (you'll find that some authors and illustrators draw their own).

AUTHOR:
Cambry
GRADE:
1

About the Author

Cambry _____
Cambry likes her family
and the colors pink and
purple and blue and
black. She really likes
her dad and her mom,
not really her brothers
and her friends are
Gracie and Lizzy.

FOLLOW-UP TEACHING:

Make copies of students' About the Author pages. Run them off on various colored
paper. Keep them in a file so they are ready when needed. Tell students to leave
space at the bottom for any information they might like to add, especially something that is pertinent to the particular book they are publishing. Around the
middle of the year, ask students if they'd like to make a new, updated version of
their page.

Short Answer (Quick Write)

★ **FOCUS:** Using logical sound-spelling to get our ideas on paper; spelling high frequency words correctly

STANDARDS CONNECTION: Writing across a varied range of time periods (some shorter, some longer); spelling unknown words phonetically, drawing on phonemic awareness and sound-spelling patterns; using conventional spelling for high-frequency words

INSTRUCTIONAL CONTEXT: The book *If You Plant A Seed* by Kadir Nelson explores the theme of kindness toward others and the fruit it bears. After reading, students were asked to think of a time when someone was kind to them. They were given limited time to write; the intent was to relay a quick personal experience that connected to the story and stayed true to the topic. Students first shared their thinking aloud, thus helping one another generate thoughts as a scaffold to writing.

TEACHING POINTS:
- Understand what to do for a Quick Write. During this short period of time, stay true to the topic given, write, and add a quick sketch, if desired, to help clarify your meaning.
- Use what you know about letters, sounds, and patterns in words to spell unknown words the way they sound using the Stretchy Hands Strategy (see page 91 for an explanation).
- Spell high-frequency words correctly in your everyday writing.

IN THIS TEXT:

Emma stays on topic, for the whole ten minutes.

> ***This morning, when I was walking, I tripped, and my sister helped me up.***

This statement is clearly on topic, given the assignment.

Emma not only wrote, but she had time to add a sketch that adds meaning to her writing.

WRITERS MIGHT CONSIDER:

Though on topic, I still have several questions I'd ask Emma: *"Where did this happen?"* and *"Did you get hurt?"* Do you have the same questions?

Even when you are writing for a short time period, it's important to reread your writing and think, *"Are there any questions readers or listeners might ask that I haven't answered?"*

IN THIS TEXT:

The ability to spell high-frequency words correctly in our everyday writing is extremely important. You don't want to have to think about how to spell these words because that will really slow your writing. Plus, you don't want to misspell them over and over because your brain will learn the wrong spellings. What can you do to make sure you write these words correctly like Emma has here, giving your brain "good" practice?

IN THIS TEXT:

Emma masterfully uses the Stretchy Hands Strategy to hear and identify the sounds in unknown words and represent them in logical ways. She also spells high-frequency words correctly since she knows these by heart. She spelled:

"wen" for *when*
logically representing all three sounds in the word

"woking" for *walking*
logically representing the first syllable and correctly spelling the last syllable *i-n-g*

"chript" for *tripped*
representing the consonant blend *tr* with *chr* which makes sense given the similarities in the sounds, spelling the chunk (rime/phonogram) *ip* correctly, and recording *t* for the last syllable (the suffix *ed*), which matches its sound (she does the same for the word *helped* on the next line)

"sistr" for *sister*
again, she has the first syllable correct, including the vowel, and represents the last syllable logically, though leaving out the vowel.

WRITERS MIGHT CONSIDER:

What strategies do you use to spell unknown words in your everyday writing? Can you describe the strategy(ies) you use?

AUTHOR:
Emma
GRADE:
1

Emma

this morning
wen I was woking
I Chript and my
sistr Helpt me
up.

This morning when I was walking I tripped and my sister helped me up.

FOLLOW-UP TEACHING:

Model the Stretchy Hands Strategy when you write in front of the class or with the class during shared, guided, and interactive writing. Watch for students using the strategy and celebrate their spellings under the document camera. Have them explain their thinking to the class or group. Additionally, if you have a Word Wall containing high-frequency words, model stopping to orally review the spelling of these words and checking them after writing. Again, celebrate students who actively use the Word Wall and who are showing that they know these words in their everyday writing.

I call my high-frequency word wall the Words We Know Wall to emphasize that these are words we know (or are trying to get to know) automatically. I encourage the use of this Wall and help students build automaticity with these words through a variety of instructional strategies. For more on this issue, see *Teaching Reading and Writing with Word Walls* (Wagstaff, 1999).

Letter

★ **FOCUS:** Writing friendly letters any time; learning the parts of a letter

STANDARDS CONNECTION: Writing friendly letters

INSTRUCTIONAL CONTEXT: We implemented the use of a mail system in the classroom. After some mini-lessons on the teaching points below, students were given the liberty to write friendly letters during any free time, when their work is done, or at home. The "postmaster" delivers the letters to students' cubbies. Students love this fun, motivating reason to write! Letters abound!

TEACHING POINTS:
- Define what friendly letters are and when they can be written.
- Identify and incorporate parts of a letter: the greeting, body, and closing.

IN THIS TEXT:

Ivy clearly knows what a friendly letter is and why to write one. She also includes some detail, not just writing one sentence saying, *You are nice!* or *I like you!*

> *You are a very nice friend to me.*

She writes to Carlee to express her kind feelings.

> *You help me with the monkey bars.*

She tells Carlee specifically why she feels she is nice.

> *Thank you for helping with the monkey bars.*

She even thanks Carlee for her help!

She includes an illustration with labels! This shows she was willing to take the time to dress up her letter to Carlee. (Look at the big smiles on the girls' faces!)

WRITERS MIGHT CONSIDER:

What are other reasons to write friendly letters? (To ask a question, make a request, invite someone to an event, etc.)

IN THIS TEXT:

Ivy clearly knows the parts of a letter and approximates their use:

> *Dear, Carlee*

She includes a friendly greeting and a comma (though it is misplaced).

Her letter has a body of three sentences.

> *Sincerely, Ivy*

She includes a friendly closing and punctuates it correctly.

WRITERS MIGHT CONSIDER:

Write a friendly letter to a classmate. Deliver it!

See the discussion of Morning Message on page 89 in the Fixer-Uppers section of "Notes."

AUTHOR:

Ivy

GRADE:

1

Dear Carlee,

You are a very nice friend to me. You help me with the monkey bars.
Thank you for helping me with the monkey bars.

Sincerely,

Ivy

FOLLOW-UP TEACHING:

Increase students' understanding of letter forms and the contexts for writing
them by using mentor texts such as *Click, Clack, Moo: Cows That Type* (Cronin)
and *Dear Peter Rabbit* (the series by Ada). Read examples of different greetings
and closings, listing these on a chart so students can refer to them in their own
letter writing. Write a letter to your class. I do this daily in the Morning Message.
Have students circle the elements of a letter and label them. Students love reading
letters from the teacher, and all kinds of teaching points can be made within.

Letter

INSTRUCTIONAL CONTEXT: This was yet another purposeful real-world reason to write! Our local community took part in a campaign to send letters to soldiers on active duty overseas. Several of our students wrote letters after learning about the military and what servicemen and women do. Teachers wrote letters alongside students, encouraging them to include details in their thank-you letters, as well as a statement or two about how knowing about the work that service people do makes them feel.

TEACHING POINTS:
- Include details in your letter. Don't just say, "Thank you." What are you thanking the person for?
- Include your feelings at the end before your closing.

IN THIS TEXT:

Michael J. includes details about what he is thanking the soldiers for:

- *Thank you for fighting for our freedom...*

- *...and our city and country...*

- *...and keeping us safe.*

WRITERS MIGHT CONSIDER:

Is there an organization or group in your community (or even far away) that provides an important service? Could you find out about this group, share information, and start your own thank-you letter campaign?

IN THIS TEXT:

Michael J. includes a simple statement about how he feels before closing his letter:

- *It makes me feel good.*

WRITERS MIGHT CONSIDER:

What is the purpose of including your feeling(s) at the end of a thank-you letter?

AUTHOR:
Michael J.
GRADE:
1

Name: Michael J

Dear Heros thank you for fighting for our freedom and our city and country and keeping us safe. It makes me feel Good. From, Michael J

Dear Heroes,

Thank you for fighting for our freedom and our city and country and keeping us safe. It makes me feel good.

From,

Michael J.

FOLLOW-UP TEACHING:

In addition to assisting students in researching a group or organization to thank in your community, you might start an in-school thank-you letter campaign. Like the friendly letter mailbox (see page 78), teach students what to do, and encourage them to write thank-you letters for anyone in the school at any time! Appreciation is important, and the art of the thank-you letter sadly seems to be fading away.

List Poetry

 FOCUS: Understanding repetition in poetry writing; choosing words that fit a topic; reading with expression to bring poetry to life

STANDARDS CONNECTION: Writing poetry; writing across genres; using verbs and adjectives (language standards)

INSTRUCTIONAL CONTEXT: We read a series of simple list poems, and practiced using expression, accompanied by actions, to make them come to life. Naturally, students wanted to try writing their own. We noted that the poems were about a single topic, moved down the page with a series of single words, and included a lot of adjectives and verbs. I modeled writing a few, using objects in the classroom as topics. Students were invited to do the same, or write about a topic of their choice.

TEACHING POINTS:
- Choose precise words that fit a topic.
- Repeat a word (or words) in a poem (or story) to create an interesting rhythmic effect.
- Read your poem with lots of expression. This brings them to life and makes writing and reading poetry so much more fun!

IN THIS TEXT:

Malakhi considered his word choice carefully, sticking to his topic:

> *roar, growl, snore*

Malakhi chose words about what lions sound like.

> *run, sleep*

Malakhi chose words about what lions do.

WRITERS MIGHT CONSIDER:

Might Malakhi have added additional words to fit his topic? I'd ask him to think of, or research, other things lions do. Would you add words to the poem if it was yours? Why or why not?

IN THIS TEXT:

Malakhi repeats the word *lions* over and over in his list poem following a pattern:

> *Lions*
> *roar*
> *Lions*
> *growl...*

WRITERS MIGHT CONSIDER:

Try writing a list poem! Think of a topic. Write down as many words about the topic as you can. You might focus on recording just adjectives or just verbs like Malakhi did. Then, follow his pattern. Write the name of your topic, then list a word underneath; repeat the topic name, list another word. Keep going until you've moved down the page in a list! Now you have a list poem!

IN THIS TEXT:

When we read Malakhi's poem, we used tremendous expression and even some action for the verbs. This made everyone, including Malakhi, more excited about his poem.

> *Lions roar* (we roared *roar*)
>
> *Lions growl* (we growled *growl*)
>
> *Lions run* (we ran in place as we read *run*)
>
> *Lions sleep* (we read *sleep* in a yawn)
>
> *Lions snore* (we added a snore and sleepily read *snore*)

WRITERS MIGHT CONSIDER:

Try reading Malakhi's poem like we did, really emphasizing the expression. Now, read it again, without the same expression. Which is better? Why do you think so? What does this mean for your future writing and reading of poetry?

AUTHOR:
Malakhi
GRADE:
1

Liyos
Liyons
ror
Liyons
gral
Liyons
run
Lixons
sleep
Lixons
snor
Lixons

Lions
Lions
roar
Lions
growl
Lions
run
Lions
sleep
Lions
snore
Lions

FOLLOW-UP TEACHING:

Reading poetry with children is a delightful way to increase their knowledge about the world, grow their love of words, and inspire them to write. When we add gusto to our reading, really using expression to the fullest, we increase their excitement to read and write exponentially. Model writing your own list poems, combine them with poems your students write, and use them for repeated shared readings! Take time for poetry breaks throughout your day!

Poetry

⭐ **FOCUS:** Observing even small happenings around us can lead to poetic expression; carefully choosing words to capture observations

STANDARDS CONNECTION: Writing poetry; writing across genres; using verbs and adjectives

INSTRUCTIONAL CONTEXT: As fall was upon us, students were asked to observe changes in the leaves for a few days and to think of words to describe what they saw. We talked about their observations and recorded adjectives, verbs, adverbs, and some simple phrases based on what they reported. I then modeled using these as starting points for drafting lines in two short poems about fall leaves. Next, they gave it a try.

TEACHING POINTS:

- Poetry helps us communicate our observations about the world to others.
- Choose precise adjectives, verbs, and adverbs to capture observations.

IN THIS TEXT:

Delilah writes a non-rhyming poem to capture her observations about fall leaves. She observed this directly and worked it into her piece.

- *red leaves*

- *bumpy, rough*

- *piling in their own piles
  in the corner of the fences*

WRITERS MIGHT CONSIDER:

Take students outside with notebooks and have them carefully observe something like the sky on a partly cloudy day or the effects of the wind blowing. Have them record any precise words that come to mind to capture what they are seeing.

Encourage them to use their notebooks outside of class, too, to capture words for other observations they make on their own.

IN THIS TEXT:

Delilah effectively uses adjectives and verbs to capture her observations about fall leaves:

> *Red leaves bumpy, rough*

She focuses her beginning just on adjectives, including some simple listing.

> *blowing off the trees
> piling in their own piles*

In this section, she focuses on verbs: what the leaves are doing, and how they are doing it. She then provides further detail about where the leaves pile in the lines that follow...

> *in the corner of the fences*

> *just to jump in!*

Delilah ends her poem focusing on action again: What do kids like to do in the leaves? Jump in!

WRITERS MIGHT CONSIDER:

Have students share the words from their outside observation. Categorize them into adjectives, verbs, and adverbs. Then, draft a poem following Delilah's pattern: Start with adjectives, followed by phrases including verbs, and perhaps some adverbs. You might end your poem like she did, by considering a personal connection or wondering about the topic.

AUTHOR:
Delilah
GRADE:
2

Fall levs
by Delilah

Red levs bumpy rough
blowing off the trees
Piling in there own piles
in the corner of the fencs
Just to jump in!

Fall Leaves
Red leaves bumpy rough
blowing off the trees
Piling in their own piles
In the corners of the fences
Just to jump in

FOLLOW-UP TEACHING:

Teach students how they can independently explore poetry by simply observing with a notebook in hand, listing words that capture observations, and then playing with them to create phrases. If you model how to work and rework a poem—reading, rearranging, and rereading possible lines—you'll give students enough ammunition to get them going as poets. Immerse them in plenty of poetry reading, as well. Be sure to celebrate their independent writing by sharing it under the document camera (including making a HUGE deal out of writing they bring in from outside of class that was completed on their own initiative).

You might like to explore my picture book *Stella: Poet Extraordinaire* to pump your students up about writing all kinds of poetry across the year.

List

★ **FOCUS:** Taking notes; publishing and presenting information

STANDARDS CONNECTION: Using a variety of digital tools to publish writing; developing speaking skills through presenting to an audience

INSTRUCTIONAL CONTEXT: Students were studying the scientific process. They were asked to observe something they wanted to learn about firsthand and then write a list of observations and record any questions about their topic that came to mind. They had prior experience with this process from observing living things in class and writing observations in their science journals. Once they had their notes they were to state some points about what they learned. Finally, students used their lists to create a presentation using Photo Story III, PowerPoint, keynote, iMovie or a tool of their choice.

TEACHING POINTS:

■ Take notes on observations and record questions. See it, then write it down using key words—not whole sentences.

■ Turn observations, questions, and conclusions into a presentation using an engaging digital format.

IN THIS TEXT:

Max chose to observe space firsthand. He wrote many notes about his observations while he looked through his telescope. He recorded key words in a list format, including some details and hypotheses, notably:

> **clouds (zoomed in)**

It was useful for him to note he zoomed in to see these.

> **color-changing rings (probably gas lines)**

He included his hypothesis about his observation.

WRITERS MIGHT CONSIDER:

Try it! What could you observe firsthand? Make a list of key words about what you see, also noting questions that come to mind. Have you learned more about your topic from this experience? How can you find the answers to these questions?

IN THIS TEXT:

Max published his information by turning his list into a PowerPoint presentation that he shared with an interest group.

Max used Google Images to find photos of Saturn, stars, clouds, and comets.

Between each picture slide he inserted a slide with a bulleted list of information from his notes. For instance:

• **Saturn has rings.**

• **Saturn's rings are made of ice and rock.**

• **Saturn has many moons.**

WRITERS MIGHT CONSIDER:

What digital tool do you know a lot about? Would you be willing to show classmates how to use it to publish writing?

AUTHOR:
Max
GRADE:
2

What I saw

- Saturn's Rings
- Stars
- Clouds – (zoomed in)
- Saturn's rings' gas
- Comet
- Color changing rings – probably gas lines.
- Saturn's moons
- Big gasses

What I Found Out

- There's lots of gasses out there in space.
- Some stars are cut– Probably when they're getting old – stars have a life span!

Space Report

What I saw

- Saturn's Rings
- Stars
- Clouds - (zoomed In)
- ~~Saturn's Ring~~ Saturn's Rings' Gas
- ~~Asteroid~~ Comet
- Color changing Rings-probably gas lines.
- Comet trails
- Saturn's Moons
- Big Gasses

What I Found Out

- There's lot's of gasses out there in space.
- Some Stars are out- Probably when they're getting old-stars have a life span!

FOLLOW-UP TEACHING:

One way to incorporate higher-level thinking is to have students take something they've written in one genre and change it to another by publishing it using digital tools. For example, if they've written an informative text, can they transform it into organized bullet points and put it into a PowerPoint presentation or key-note using photos or images? Think of the processes involved in this kind of task. Students need to distinguish key information, think about how to organize it, and then consider how to present it. It sounds involved, but it's actually very doable and, because of the digital tools, very motivating and fun.

Teachers who are hesitant to use digital publishing tools with students might try using one at a time. They can get students started using a tool even when they, the teacher, have only the most basic knowledge. Then, the kids themselves can lead the way by asking and answering questions for each other. It's very engaging and often leads to surprising results.

88

You are a verey nice friend to me. You help me with meunky bars. Thank you for helping with the meunky bars.

Sincerly, Ivy

Notes

Fixer-Uppers

Over the years, I've developed some tried-and-true methods for fixing up common K–2 writing issues. Let's start with one of my pet peeves:

IRREGULAR HIGH-FREQUENCY WORDS

How can we get students to spell irregular high-frequency words correctly in their everyday writing? I cringe when I see students writing the wrong spelling for words like *the, said, you,* and *what* over and over again in their everyday writing. If they constantly write these words incorrectly, they learn the wrong spellings.

There's an easy solution to this: create and use a Words We Know Wall (Wagstaff, 1999). Each day I write a Morning Message to my students. The Message becomes a context for lots of teaching, and we also use it as a context for mining high-frequency, irregularly spelled words. We start by adding words to our Words We Know Wall that we see over and over again in the Message. I use a three-panel display board or a flat foam board for the Wall, which I label alphabetically.

A first grade "Words We Know Wall" (in progress) on two pieces of foam board from the dollar store. Note that this teacher added some soundable high-frequency words, too.

Once a word has come up repeatedly, and we've studied the spelling by dot-checking (putting a dot under each letter as it is spelled aloud, causing students to look at *each and every* letter) and repeatedly circling the word in the Message, I write the word on a card and add it to the Wall alphabetically. Once a word is added, students know they must spell this word correctly in their writing all the time. I have them use the Circling Things We Know editing strategy (pages 22–23) to check their spellings. When I'm conferencing, if I see a word from the Wall that's misspelled, I have the child fix it, or I put a dot at the end of the line. He must then reread to find the high-frequency word that is misspelled and make the correction.

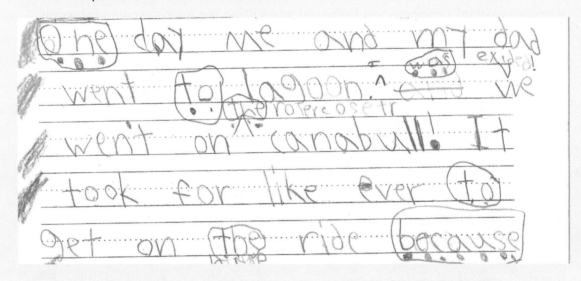

Circling Things We Know and dot-checking to check irregular high-frequency word spellings

Since these words are high frequency, we write and read them often. Thus, the *perfect* practice-makes-perfect strategy of using the Wall as a constant scaffold helps students truly learn and become automatic with the correct spellings. I refer to the Wall during modeled writing, and students refer to it during shared and interactive writing. Since they use it daily as they write independently, as well, it all adds up to a multitude of repeated correct exposures. We know, and research confirms, that this is what results in permanent learning. In kindergarten, we add just 15 to 20 of these words during the year, while in first and second grade, I work with the students to add about 40 of these words over time. They leave second grade with the words down pat. Problem solved.

SPELLING

Students' spelling can be a real sticking point! What to do? As I'm sure you are aware, spellers move through predictable stages (Bear, et al., 2011; Henderson, 1990; Gentry, 1982). Knowing these stages, and how to push students' development forward, is critical to making a real difference in their everyday writing. I modify my teaching of the Stretchy Hands Strategy to meet students where they are as spellers. See kindergartner Gracie's text on page 34 and first-grader Emma's text on page 76 for some examples.

Claire stretches her fists apart as she slowly segments the word "fit". As she voices each sound, she moves her head from left to right, stopping for each. She records a letter for each sound as she moves along.

The idea behind the Stretchy Hands Strategy is to teach spelling strategies that students can use *while* writing. I don't just give students lists of words to study and practice and then give the Friday test. They need to know, practice, and use *strategies* for coming up with logical spellings for words they don't know as they write in varied contexts. In conjunction with the Stretchy Hands Strategy, which I love because it is concrete and involves a kinesthetic element, I implement Challenge Words as part of our weekly routine.

Challenge Words provides students with explicit, guided practice in using spelling strategies to spell unknown words, accompanied by immediate feedback. I explain that we all come to words we don't know how to spell as we write. But we have to have strategies we can use to get those words down on paper, to give them our best shot, so we can use the words we choose (not just those we know how to spell) and get on with our writing rather than remaining stuck. I model and think-aloud strategically, connecting to words I know to help me spell new words or word parts. I use our phonics Word Walls (Name/ABC Wall or Chunking Wall) to make analogies. Then, I pose a word that I know will provide some challenge to students and I tell everyone to give it a go on their papers using the same strategies I modeled. Everyone gives the word a try. I circulate and write down a few different variations of the attempts on the board. We then discuss each attempt: What is logical about this attempt? What did this speller do that makes sense for this word? Students know the goal is not necessarily to get the word right but, instead, to give it a good, logical try using what we know.

For example, in fall in kindergarten, a challenge word might be *spot*. Student attempts might include: *s, s-t*, and *s-p-t*. I write these on the board, then run my finger under each and give specific feedback for everyone to hear.

> For *s*, "You can see this speller was able to listen inside the word *spot* to hear the first sound. He may have connected to /s/ /s/ *Sam* on the Name Wall, or maybe he automatically knew he needed the letter *s* for the /s/ /s/ sound. Good job! That's a start!

> For *s-t*, "This speller was able to hear the beginning and ending sounds in the word *spot*. She has the letter *s* for /s/, then heard that /t/ /t/ sound at the end, just like the word we know /t/ /t/ *to*. Yep, the /t/ /t/ sound is represented by the letter *t*!

> For *s-p-t*, "This speller was able to stretch the word even more /s/ /p/ /ot/. See how she began the spelling with *s-p-*? Let's all stretch the word slowly. Put your Stretchy Hands up by your mouth. Now say the beginning part slowly, stretching the sounds (students move their hands apart as they segment /s/ /p/). See how our mouths moved from /sssss/ to /ppppp/?

She knew she needed the letter *p* for that second sound. She has the ending sound, too. /spt/ /spt/ s-p-t. That is a good attempt at the word *spot*. Now watch me."

I model stretching the word orally, moving my stretchy hands apart as I segment, exaggerating my mouth movements and writing a letter down for each sound. I always end the lesson by showing the correct spelling.

In fall in second grade, an appropriate challenge word might be *hiccup*. I teach students to clap the word to break it into syllables and to write a line for each chunk to remind them of each part they need to spell. They write the letters for the syllables on the lines (See the poster on page 94). Then, they attack the spelling one small chunk at a time while making connections to words they know. Again, I circulate and write two or three different student attempts on the board. Then, I run my finger under each and provide feedback while everyone watches, thus reinforcing good spelling strategies.

If one attempt is *hkup*, I might say, "I see this speller heard the beginning and ending sound in the first syllable, /h/ /k/ and connected to the right letters. *H-k* is a good attempt for /hic/. But, we have to remember, *every* syllable, *every* chunk, has a vowel. Good attempt, though. For the last chunk she heard /up/ and spelled it just like the little word we all know: *u-p*."

If a different attempt is *hikup*, I respond, "This is another good attempt. *H-i-k* makes sense for /hic/, and this speller remembered the vowel /i/ /i/ i like the word on our Wall: *itch*. Usually the *ick* chunk is spelled *i-c-k* like *sick* or *trick*. He was also able to easily spell the ending chunk /up/ *u-p*. That makes good sense."

I then model and think aloud, "I hear /hic/ (drawing a line for that syllable), and I'd probably try this chunk like other words I know with *h-i-c-k*. Then, the *up* chunk is easy, (drawing a line for that syllable) *u-p*. You know what? This word actually has an odd spelling. The first syllable is *h-i-c*, not *i-c-k* like most words, and the second syllable is *c-u-p*; *h-i-c-c-u-p*. A writer could really get hung up on this word, but since you know what to do, that won't happen to you. Use your strategies, make a good attempt, and move on, getting your ideas down."

It should take only seven to ten minutes to work on two or three Challenge Words. We do these lessons right before Writing Workshop or independent writing. At the beginning of the year, I do them three times a week. Then, as students' skills grow, I cut back. They also fit for small-group lessons, and I prompt students to use the same strategies we've practiced if they come to me for spelling help while writing throughout the day. (For much more about Challenge Words and lessons like it, see Wagstaff, 2009, 2011, and 2016. You can also see these sources for more about the Name/ABC Wall and the Chunking Wall.)

For emergent spellers:

When Trying to Spell a Word, I Can...

1. Say the word slowly.

2. Stretch the word. Count the sounds.

3. Draw a line for each sound.

4. Write letter(s) for each sound.

5. CHECK IT!
   Run my finger under it and blend.
   Does it sound right?
   Does it look right?

For more developed spellers:

When Trying to Spell a Hard Word, I Can...

1. Say the word slowly.

2. Break the word into chunks.

3. Work <u>one</u> chunk at a time:
   Use word parts I know.
   Remember a <u>vowel</u> in each chunk.

4. CHECK IT!
   Run my finger under and blend the chunks.
   Does it sound right?
   Does it look right?

Reprinted with permission from *The Common Core Companion: Booster Lessons, Grades K–2: Elevating Instruction Day by Day* (Wagstaff, 2016)
Artistic credit: Mel Lloyd of Graphics From the Pond http://www.fromthepond.com.au/

PUNCTUATION AND CONVENTIONS

You might be asking yourself, "How can we get students to use correct capitalization, end marks, and other conventions that we've taught in their everyday writing?" Lucio's sample (page 22) shows part of how I deal with this issue. I teach my students to Circle Things We Know in their writing with the support of a Help Wall (Wagstaff, 1999). The Help Wall is built on a foam or display board like my other Word Walls. It has categories for the conventions and language usage skills we teach such as: When to Use Capitals, Putting in Punctuation, Homophones, and Contractions.

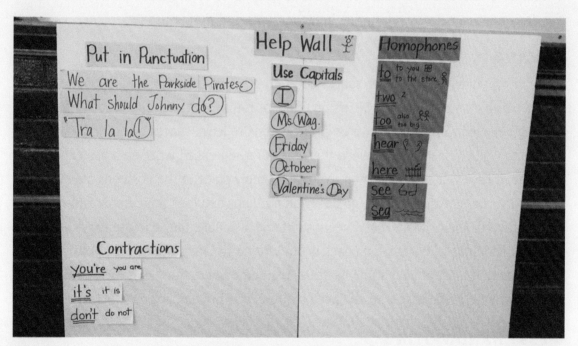

The Help Wall is a constant support to writers. Here you see one in progress on two pieces of foam board. It is built over time when conventions have been adequately taught. Depending on students' needs, other categories can be added.

Over time, we mine examples from the Morning Message and other reading contexts. For example, we note how sentences end differently depending on their purposes. We place references on the Help Wall to remind us of what we've learned. The students and I pick short sentences from favorite books to be referents for different end marks. (Using sentences from favorite books provides a memorable context that students can relate to. This helps them make more neural connections, solidifying learning.)

So, **"What should Johnny do?"** from *One Was Johnny* (Sendak) becomes our reference for using a question mark and **"Tra la la!"** from *Captain Underpants* (Pilkey) becomes our reference for using an exclamation mark. When students are asked to Circle Things We Know in their writing, we first review the references on the Wall. I model using the Wall to help me remember what I know in my writing such as which spelling for *to*, *two*, or *too* is appropriate (homophones have little sketches or phrases next to them to help students remember the correct usage). Also, I routinely have students pair up with peers to check for these items in their writing. These ideas are simple, don't take a lot of time or effort, and they really work! Remember to celebrate students' efforts under the document camera as you notice improvements and proper usage.

SPACING

Many of my students don't leave spaces between their words when they write. Refer to Jacob's opinion text on page 38. Using Cheerios is a fun way to teach and reinforce spacing between words. I further prompt my writers to leave spaces by posting a visual. (I simply glue Cheerios in between the words of a sentence I write on a poster.) As I circulate, if I see students forgetting to space, I simply point to the poster as a reminder. This is a cue that they need to go back and put lines between their words and space going forward. Again, if you keep Cheerios out and available, they can use those as they proceed. Additionally, when we go back in our writing to Circle Things We Know, we can circle spaces. If most of your students get to the point where they've mastered this skill, you can privately tell those who still need reinforcement to go back and circle their spaces.

MESSY HANDWRITING

Many children have messy handwriting. To correct that, we need to start by teaching them proper pencil-gripping skills and purchase rubber or plastic pencil grippers to help children develop the habit of holding their pencils correctly. This helps a great deal and is worth the time and money since we are developing lifelong habits.
We also need to teach handwriting—short, quick lessons on letter formation should be included in our schedules, especially at the beginning of the year. I always combine my handwriting lessons with another skill: in kindergarten, letter naming and review of

the Name/ABC Wall followed by rainbow writing the letter(s) we just practiced using proper formation and strokes; in first and second grades, blending simple words with easy chunks from our Chunking Wall, then practicing writing the letters in the chunks with proper formation and strokes.

Often students with messy handwriting form their letters from the bottom up. In other words, they start at the baseline and work toward the mid or top lines. This is a no-no. Such habits not only affect how the letters are formed, but they significantly slow writers down. We constantly say a refrain such as, "Letters always rain down" as we practice letter formation. I can then use this as a prompt when I see students working bottom up.

Naturally, part of improving handwriting is developing fine-motor skills. These skills should develop naturally as students engage in varied play and school activities, including daily writing. However, if you see a child with handwriting that is consistently far worse than peers, and you've intervened as best you can, look into having him checked by an occupational therapist.

LETTER REVERSALS

Letter reversals are common in young writers and should correct themselves by the end of second grade, as long as students are writing daily. This doesn't mean, however, that we can't give students feedback and practice along the way. Here's what I do. When I see a student making consistent reversals of the same letter, I place a small sticky note with the letter on her desk, then have her turn her paper over to the back and write the letter correctly down the side. If need be, I put my hand over her hand and help her form the letter properly. Then, I ask her to refer to her sticky note in her everyday writing, looking especially closely for this letter when she Circles Things We Know.

General Guidelines

We'll switch gears now. Here you'll find general tips that I find provide useful guidance for working with K–2 writers.

SCAFFOLDING STRUGGLING WRITERS

Group writing first One method I use to provide extra support is to *first* engage young writers in shared or interactive writing about our topic, working on one piece cooperatively over the course of a few days. We read and reread as we go, refer to our Word Walls, and use our Stretchy Hands to help spell unknown words. When we finish our group piece, I invite everyone to then write their *own* pieces on the topic so they can take it home to share what we've learned. Youngsters are eager to do this so they can show what they know. Since we've already worked on a piece together, they have that experience to draw upon for success, applying the same skills and strategies we practiced together.

An alternative to this is to have those who are ready go ahead and write on their own while you invite those who need extra support to work with you to compose using shared or interactive writing. Shared and interactive writing combined with a small(er) group setting make for a more supportive experience.

Who's ready to write? After I complete a writing lesson I ask students, "Who's ready to write?" Those who are ready are off and running. Those who are not stay on the rug with me so I can further support them through reteaching or talking-out ideas. As students in this small group get what they need, they go back to their areas and write. If one or two students are really struggling, I can assist them at their seats through interactive writing, providing sentence frames or key words, or by having them walk the room and watch what other writers are doing.

Talk-it-out As you read several of the mentor texts, you'll notice we talk-it-out to scaffold writing. This can be done with or without a graphic organizer. The idea is to capitalize on the fact that young students are often better with oral language than with written language. So, if we tease out our thinking by talking out what we want to write before writing it, the task of writing becomes easier. Using keyword notes on a graphic organizer, for example, I model talking-out my ideas in whole sentences. Students listen and give me a thumbs up or down as I go, sentence by sentence. ("Does this sound right? Does it sound like a whole sentence?")

I often model starting and restarting, stating and restating, to demonstrate how to work something orally until I feel ready to write. I gradually release this process to students, finding they have great success talking-out their writing to a peer or to themselves. I invite volunteers to come forward and talk-it-out in front of the class, receiving feedback from their peers as to whether they have complete sentences (thumbs up) or not (thumbs down). When they don't, we assist. Hint: For those who need more support, have them talk-out one section or one sentence at a time, and then have them write. This chunks the task, making it simpler. Provide even more help by making a blank for each word a student will write after she rehearses a sentence with you. Giving students a visual to work from, such as a list of key words, Thinking Boxes, columned notes, or other graphic organizers, greatly helps.

Dictation For students who struggle mightily, it is perfectly fine to have them occasionally dictate their stories or ideas to you as you type them. Print the pages so they can read and share them with others. If you've helped them record a story, have them illustrate it and bind it into a book. They need to feel the joy of sharing something polished and special. This can be hugely motivating and boost their willingness to put forth extra effort as they learn to write.

Use technology For those who are really struggling, give them the option of talking-it-out into an iPad or other device. They can play it back as they write it down. Another option is to use voice-to-text technology for assistance. Sometimes just seeing the words flow onto the page can be very encouraging and push students forward.

TAKE A BALANCED APPROACH TO WRITING

Give students balanced writing experiences across genres and forms.

Be sure students have opportunities to write across genres so they experience different structures and purposes. Don't neglect narrative writing even though it may not be included on formal tests. Don't forget forms of writing that may not be articulated in your standards such as: poetry, letter writing, journaling, the writing of lists, reminder notes, jots for studies across the curriculum, quick writes, etc. We want students to understand that writers write across the day for varied reasons—not just in school.

Use a combination of writing modes: modeled writing, shared writing, interactive writing, and independent writing.

As with reading, different writing modes provide different benefits for students. I wouldn't want to short-change any of them because I don't want to short-change the varied ways I can support my students' writing development.

During **modeled writing**, teachers are the writers. They do all the work. They think aloud, talking about what they are doing as they compose in front of the class. Over time, as students listen and watch, they learn the strategies writers use while composing different types of texts. Model writing frequently. Students learn the ins and outs of the writing process as they see and hear the thinking and writing develop right in front of them in real time as you, a fellow writer, value, struggle, problem-solve, and persevere. (For more on modeled writing, see my book *Quick Start to Writing Workshop Success*.)

During **shared writing**, the teacher and students negotiate together what will be written, talking-out their content, giving it a try on paper, and making changes as they go. The teacher is the one who does the physical writing. This way, students can focus all their attention on content without worrying about spelling or mechanics (unless the teacher poses a question or prompts such discussion).

In contrast, during **interactive writing**, the teacher *and* students do the physical writing. The content is still negotiated jointly, but as students "share the pen," they grapple with spelling and mechanics, thus working on their phonological awareness and phonics skills. (Since interactive writing promotes growth in these areas and does so within the meaningful act of writing, it is a staple in my K–2 classrooms.) In both shared and interactive writing, students have more responsibility for the writing than they do with modeled writing, but scaffolding and support are always available since the teacher is actively involved. In essence, these are forms of guided practice. (Another one of my books has detailed information on interactive writing: *Using Name Walls to Teach Reading and Writing.*)

Obviously, students need opportunities to try out all they are learning independently, so having time in the day for Writing Workshop or independent writing is critical. Students will approximate the use of the strategies they've seen modeled and have tried during guided experiences. Though the teacher may be available to provide some support, it's important that students grapple with the act of composing on their own or with some assistance from peers. Teachers look closely at what their students are producing to help them determine next steps in their instruction.

Even our youngest, most emergent writers must have daily independent writing time. If they are not given this time, how will they develop their skills? They might begin by drawing and labeling or scribbling down letters, but the more teachers model and involve them in shared and interactive writing, the more they will grow. Naturally, the instruction they receive in phonological awareness, phonics, spelling, and vocabulary will also push their development as writers, especially when they are given daily opportunities to apply it!

Balance assigned writing with choice writing.

Students need opportunities to write on topics of their choosing. They need to know how to generate their own ideas and keep a running list (See Cynesha's text on page 73). If we assign everything they write, they are not learning the range of skills and strategies otherwise possible: How do I come up with my own ideas to write about? What if I want to write something I've never tried before? What can I do to research my own questions? What might I do with my choice writing? Giving students choice feeds their motivation to write.

Balance formal and informal writing.

Much of what young students write should be informal, meaning they don't go through all the steps in the writing process to complete a perfectly published piece. Just as with reading, students need to accumulate "miles on the page," applying their skills and strategies to write as best they can, and engaging in lots of writing daily. If we correct all their errors and force them to rewrite in an attempt for perfection, we won't be allowing them enough practice. We don't take this approach to reading! We don't sit across from them and correct every word they read, yet they still develop and thrive. We need to remember to approach writing the same way.

MAKE WRITING PURPOSEFUL AND RELEVANT

The more purposeful and relevant your writing experiences are, the more engaged and motivated your writers will be. As I plan writing experiences for my students I think, Why are we doing this? Why should students care? This often leads me to a purpose. Plus, real reasons to write come up daily, even without planning. For example, if the principal announces a change in lunchroom procedure and students groan, have them discuss, then write, their opinions about it. Deliver their pieces to the principal. Or, if students come up with questions while we're reading or observing, there's a real reason to investigate and write.

LET THEIR VOICES BE HEARD

Provide multiple opportunities for students to share their writing with others. Informal peer-to-peer sharing in the classroom counts. But, also consider having students share beyond your classroom walls. They might share their writing with the school over the intercom, post pieces in the hallway and invite comments, publish a book and put it in the school library for check-out, publish on the Internet, send letters to faculty members, classrooms, a business, or a children's book author, perform pieces for a parent audience, or bring their pieces to the classroom next door to pair-up and share. Even the simplest forms of sharing, like reading a bit of their piece to the teacher, are important. Writers need to feel their ideas matter and their voices are valued. Take time to share and celebrate. When you see how students react, you won't regret a minute of it.

Teaching Points Matrix

	Author	Grade	Teaching Points
Informative	Claire	K	naming and supplying info on a topic
			staying on topic
			revising to add a detail
	Cale	K	beginning writing with a topic sentence or phrase
			writing to a tight topic
	Katelyn	1	organizing information around main ideas or categories
			clearly introducing the topic
	Michael	1	using text features including bold headings
			using diagrams and labels
	Hailey	1	using temporal words in procedural writing
			clearly introducing the topic
	Lucio	1	editing for conventions and mechanics by "Circling Things We Know'
			organizing procedural writing
	Ainslee	1	answering who, what, why questions using more than one source
			including a purposeful conclusion
	Andy	2	using a graphic organizer to prepare for writing (2 column notes)
			using key words to remember ideas, then recording them in your own language
			talking-out our writing using a graphic organizer prepares us to write
	Adrian	2	using a question/answer organizational structure
			incorporating voice
			using content-specific vocabulary
	Kinsley	2	starting a piece in an attention-grabbing way
			using varied beginnings for sentences (pronouns)
Opinion	Gracie	K	communicating through drawing and writing, using the Stretchy Hands Strategy
			including details in one's drawing to augment meaning
	Nevaeh	K	using a graphic organizer (Thinking Boxes)
			stating one's opinion on a *topic*, including one reason for the opinion
			presenting to an audience
	Jacob	K	spacing between words
			using end mark punctuation
	Emma	1	beginning opinions with signal phrases
			supplying at least one reason for an opinion
	Colby & Brenna	1	borrowing language from one another's writing
			including a purposeful conclusion
	Max	2	directly stating one's opinion about *text*
			supplying explicit reasons for one's opinion
	Aiden	2	writing opinions for real purposes
			supporting one's opinion with text evidence
	John	2	writing opinions for real purposes
			using transitions to connect ideas
			using linking words to connect opinion and reasons

	Author	Grade	Teaching Points
Narrative	Felix	K	using drawing to get your writing on paper
			labeling your drawing(s) to augment meaning
	Molly	K	focusing on a single event in a personal narrative
			including characters, a setting, and what happened
			showing story elements in words and illustration(s)
	Violet	K	including characters in a fictional narrative
			including fictional happenings in a fictional narrative
	Ruby	1	planning stories and making additions using a graphic organizer (Thinking Boxes)
			talking-out one's writing as a scaffold
	Tayvin	1	focusing on word choice
			writing long
	Caden	2	revising to change content and answering questions asked by others
			rereading to ensure revisions sound right and are correctly placed
	Gabe	2	focusing one's story on a small moment within a series of events
			adding details related to thoughts and feelings
	Daysen	2	including a clear beginning, middle, and end in a story
			using dialogue
Other Text Types	Brennan	K	knowing what to do on a poetry walk
			turning sketches/notes into a poem
	Cynesha	1	keeping a personal Topics List; always listening and looking for writing ideas
			stretching ourselves as writers to try different genres
	Cambry	1	knowing the purpose and structure of an About The Author page
			including relevant information in an About The Author page
	Emma	1	knowing what to do during a Quick Write
			spelling strategically (use the Stretchy Hands Strategy effectively)
			spelling high-frequency words correctly in everyday writing
	Ivy	1	writing friendly letters any time
			including the elements of a letter: greeting, body, closing
	Michael J.	1	including details in a thank-you letter
			including one's feelings in a letter
	Malakhi	1	choosing precise words to fit a topic
			repeating words or phrases in poetry to achieve an interesting effect
			reading with expression
	Delilah	2	communicating our observations about the world to others through poetry
			choosing precise words to describe our observations (using adjectives, verbs, adverbs)
	Max	2	writing a list to keep notes on observations and to record questions
			publishing using digital tools

References

Bear, D., M. Invernizzi, S. Templeton, and F. Johnston. 2011. *Words Their Way: Word Study for Phonics, Vocabulary, and Spelling Instruction* (5th Edition). Upper Saddle River, NJ: Pearson.

Gentry, J. R. " An Analysis of Developmental Spelling in GNYS AT WRK." *The Reading Teacher* 36. 1982: 192-200.

Henderson, E. 1990. *Teaching Spelling*. Boston, MA: Houghton Mifflin.

Hoyt, L. 2011 *Crafting Nonfiction Primary: Lessons on Writing Process, Traits, and Craft (grades K–2)*. Portsmouth, NH: FirstHand, Heinemann.

Kisloski, C., and J. Feldman. 2015. *Dr. Jean's Reading Recipes*. Peterborough, NH: SDE Professional Development Resources.

Oxenhorn, A., and L. Calkins. 2003. *Small Moments: Personal Narrative Writing*. Portsmouth, NH: Heinemann.

Rogers, T., and A. Feller. 2016. "Discouraged by Peer Excellence: Exposure to Exemplary Peer Performance Causes Quitting." *Psychological Science* Online First, published on January 29, 2016 as doi:10.1177/0956797615623770.

Wagstaff, J.M. 1999. *Teaching Reading and Writing with Word Walls*. New York: Scholastic.

———. 2009. *Using Name Walls to Teach Reading and Writing*. New York: Scholastic.

———. 2011. *Quick Start to Writing Workshop Success*. New York: Scholastic.

———. 2015. *Stella and Class: Information Experts*. Peterborough, NH: SDE Professional Development Resources.

———. 2015. *Stella: Poet Extraordinaire*. Peterborough, NH: SDE Professional Development Resources.

———. 2015. *Stella Tells Her Story*. Peterborough, NH: SDE Professional Development Resources.

———. 2015. *Stella Writes an Opinion*. Peterborough, NH: SDE Professional Development Resources.

———. 2016. *The Common Core Companion: Booster Lessons, Grades K–2: Elevating Instruction Day by Day*. Thousand Oaks, CA: Corwin.

The Mentor Texts

Date April 14

Dear Aunt Lucy,

I'm so excited to share my story with you! I've spent a lot of time working on it in school, coming up with an idea to write about, sharing it aloud, planning my story, writing it, and sharing it with my classmates to make it better and better. Now I have a story I'm proud of. I hope you enjoy reading it!

Please take a minute to write me a quick note telling me what you liked about my story. It doesn't have to be long—just a few sentences would be great. This will further encourage me to continue writing.

Thank you so much!

Sincerely,

Stella

claire

a frog

Frog's can hop they have web feet they doz the web feet to sime.

Cale ___/___/___

I lrnd that

only sed sgro.

Katelyn

I take dance at Jazz dance Studio.
I dance on Mondays and Thursdays.
I take Tap Hip hop Jazz
and Acro I like to dance!
In tap class I wear tap shoes.
Miss Mary teashes us to
shufle and to kick ball
Change.
Miss Carly teashes Hip hop
She takes counts we dance to
the counts. Mr Murphy he
teaches Hip hop too.
Acro is streching and tumbling
I can do a back bend.
And Jazz is streching and
doing a dance. I like dance!

black jagwoue

Name: Michael G

<u>Habitat:</u> `America. So th

ther are a lot

of trees.

Its watem.

ther are dens.

<u>Looks:</u>

The black

jagwor has

black fre.

The back jagwor

has black

spos.

I chose the
black jackware
becauese They
can blin in
The shat os.

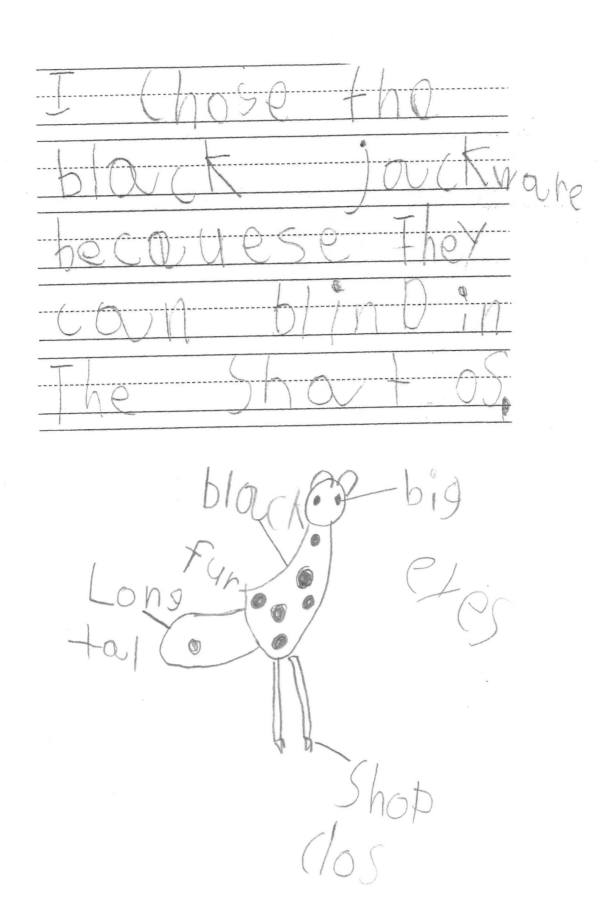

black   big

fur

Long   eyes

tal

Shop

clos

What I do in the
winter I bild a smowman
a girl smowman with
my dad. First we put
snow for her bodie. Second
we put a carret for her nose
and we put buttens for her
eyes. third we put a hat on the
Snowman. I love bilding snowmen.

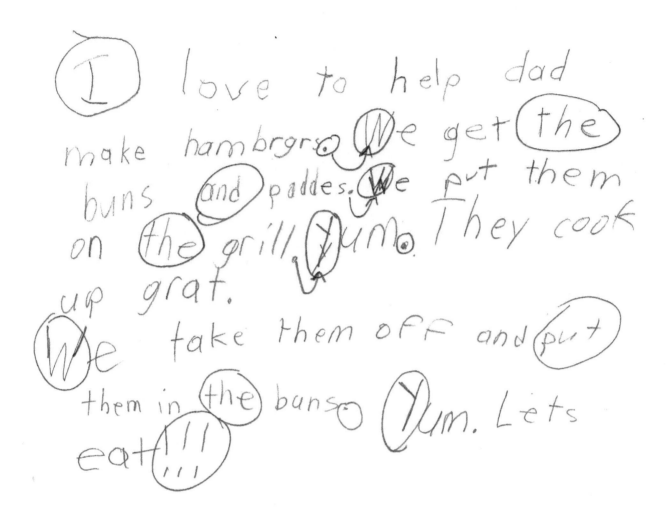

I love to help dad make hambrgrs. We get the buns and paddes. We put them on the grill. Yum. They cook up grat.

We take them off and put them in the buns. Yum. Lets eat!!!!

The Nice Boy

Jack Stevenson was a nice boy. He helpt the plees day Delta by Seling snow cons because he was nice

unuf to do that. Dont you thenk you can do sumthing like that.

use imagination | change the work

1. boxes tape = arcade 2. cardard challeng
2 1st game ✓ miny
Baskiball

Every october
1 ✓ Summr vacation 1 Video caine wanted
6 ✓ fun pas oliy $2 Peple to Make there
3 his ✓ games got onen staf.
bigr and beter

2 seint

✓ 4 soccer
game and pepeler
side it was te esay
then he made it
harder. 5 He mode
hes one shrt!

Tonadoes

Woah! I see a Tonadoe Aaaaaa! It is ging

to hit us. It is omost here! Help Me! Waht do you

do wen a tonadoe is here? You find seltter.

Don't go by windos because it will hurt you.

It will destroy houses.

What kinds of tornados are there? A rope tornad

is like a rope and they are skinny. Theres a

waterspout tonadoe, a waterspout is a tonadoe

that can go on water.

A wedge tornado is the biggest tornado.

What is a tornado? A tornado has lightning.

It has rain. It is like a funnle. I dont like tornados

because they destroy everything.

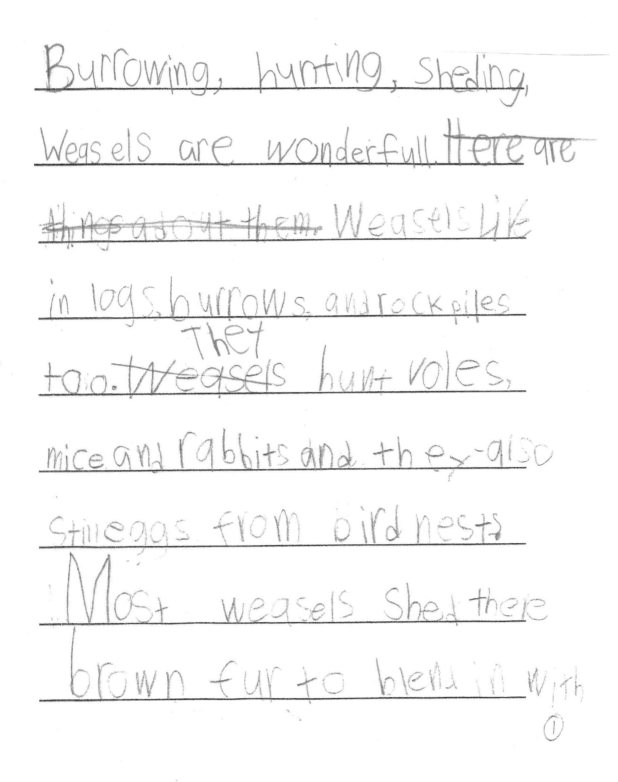

Burrowing, hunting, sheding, Weasels are wonderfull. Here are ~~things about them.~~ Weasels like in logs, burrows, and rock piles too. They ~~Weasels~~ hunt voles, mice and rabbits and they ~~also~~ still eggs from bird nests. Most weasels shed there brown fur to blend in with

①

the snow. They turn white! They go hed first with there long bodies into tiny burrows to sleep, live and hunt. ~~snow~~ They also start to hunt when they are two munts old I want to see a weasel.

Gracie

Novaeh
Best

Be

BK
myge R Hvu Bedl

Jacob

I! like! Wintr!
I like Wintr beKus
I here Snobol
fits. I like Wintr
beKus I go sledeng.

Dear   Jack

I   think

that   you

made   a   good

dashshin. I   like

your   dasishin

because   you helpt

your   community.

from   Emma

I Wihs we cahe
have saming elnfs
then milk.
becauss milk
is gros. hos
with me.

My opinion is that we should have more home work because then We lern who is with me?

I want to read Geronimo Stilton: Lost Treasure Of The Emerald Eye Because it's the First book of the series, And because I like to read books in order. Last, I read on the back that they found a treasure map somewhere, and they want to find the treasure. That sounds exciting!

Dear mrs. Harris,

I rely hope you can get this book Dog vs. cat by Chris Gall. One reson is because at the end the cat said "what is that?" the dog poopt. A baby moved in ther room and they said "it stinks. oh, the smell!

The crecher never stops skreching."
Then they desided to move out.
Also, their behaveyor was silly becaue they got echether in trubol like when the cat bloows the dog wisol to make the dog howl and the

dog Put cat nip on the sofa and the cat tore all the sofa UP!

mrs. Harris ples get this book for the school.

From, Aiden

Dear Mr. Stevenson,

This is John Dorius. I am writing to you with my opinion. I think that we should leave the 100s club posters up in the hall all year. Here's why. A few months ago, I made the 100s club finally after waiting a very long time. It was around the end of the month. I was so excited to have my name on that poster. I brought my grandma in to show her that I'd finally made the club.

But, since it was so close to the end of the month, the poster was only up a few days. I went to look at it again, and my name was gone. I felt bad and sad. I think it would be better to leave the posters up all year since kids work so hard to get to be part of the club. This way, they can feel proud and be happy about their accomplishment all year long.

Sincerely,

John Dorius

Violet

OWon day I
Was sWmen
Then Ichnd
Intoo a mrmad
I like It. I avd
It. thenIehloo

to the Syn!

UP

UP

UP UP

Ph 100

I

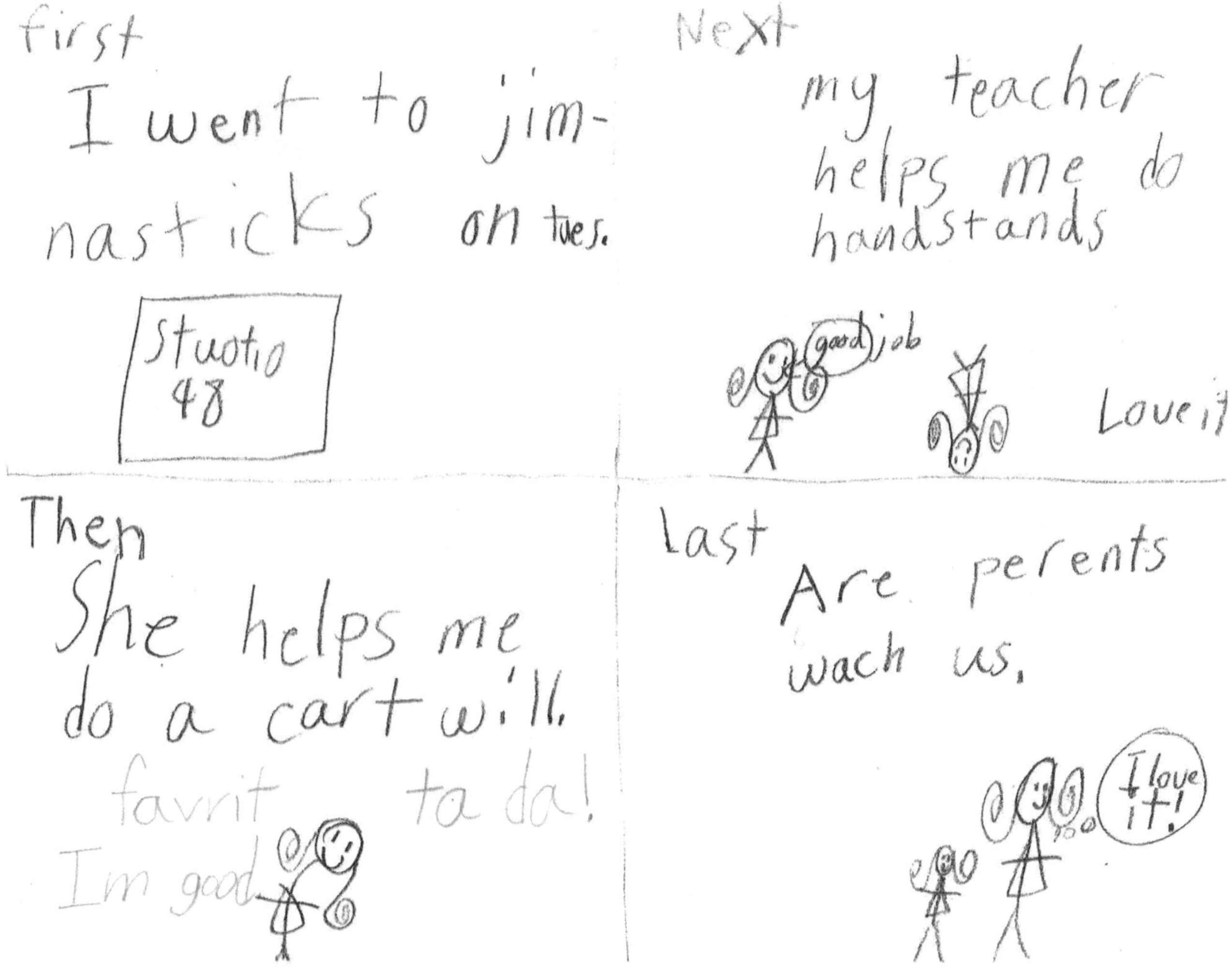

first
I went to jim-
nasticks   on tues.

stuotio
48

Next
my teacher
helps me do
handstands

good job

Love it

Then
She helps me
do a cart will.
favrit   ta da!
I'm good

Last
Are perents
wach us.

I love
it!

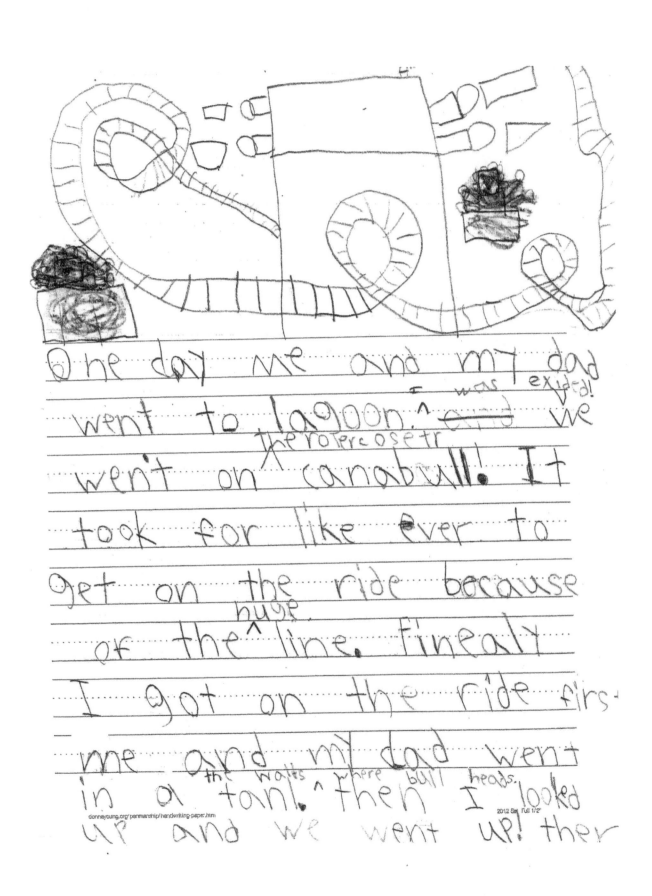

One day me and my dad
went to lagoon. ^I was exited! and we
went on ^the rollercosetr canabull! It
took for like ever to
get on the ride because
of the ^huge line. Finealy
I got on the ride firs-
me and my dad went
in a tanl. ^the walls ^there bull heads. I looked
up and we went up! ther

when we got to the top
it went crazy fast then
the ride was over! I
got off and I wanted
to go 50 times more!

Caden

One morning, I went to the
airport. When I got to the
When i woke up
With my friends.   becuase it was my first time
airport I was exited. But When
I got on the airplane, I felt
to florida When we got off
the airplane
sick. But after, it was fun. We
we got in the air it was fun.
went on a boat to the bhahamas.
I did not like the boat ride. And

I. did not feel good I felt like I could barf. My freind got sick like me. When We got to the bhahamas I swam in the ocean. It was fun. My favorite part of the trip was when I swam in the ocean. I saw corole and fish. I liked the green blue corole and fish. they were prety.

I went camping in the mountains with my dad. We were going fishing very clos to the watr. We wated a long time to get a fish. It was so boring! It seemed like forever. Finaly we gote a littl fish. Woo hoo! We cut the scin off so anather fish wold eat the scin. Then we cot a big fish. And we ckooct it and ate it. Ick! I downt like the tast of fish but it was still fun!

We Can Do This! by Janiel Wagstaff. ©2017. Taylor & Francis Group.

Daysen
by

The night the legos came
to life

I was buliding with my legos

when mom came in and said

"Time for bed!" I went to bed.

when mom was asleep I

herd something. eeck! my

door opend. I got a littel

scared. when I saw my legos

walking acrost my door!

I wisperd "wow this is epic.

M

Sudenly my legos spoded me! I hid under my covers. "you don't have to bes card. said Lego

Emit.

"I don't?" I said. "you don't.

"We all are friends," said lego batman. "Cool!" I said. "ya. we can stay up late." I said "Hawe can," said the lego. "awsome." I said. "this is gung begreat

E.
I said, wewached
goos bumps, Starwars
and scary movies. We played
video games. It was.
~~ausom.~~ epic Evry night the legos
would come to life. the End

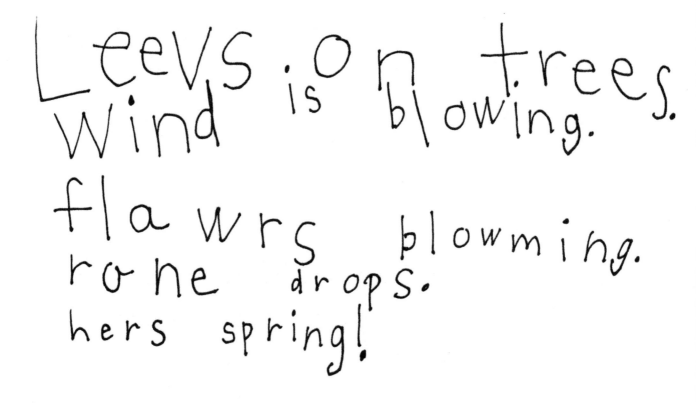

Leevs on trees.
Wind is blowing.
flawrs blowming.
rone drops.
hers spring!

best   pet ✔

grama cookees making

letr   to   Ashlee ✔

Kamluns!   info   book

favret   sport —jimnastks

RuLES! for game ✔

book   Postr   READ click clack moo
crains   Poem

About the Author

I ♥ You
mom and
Dad

camdry
Camdry likes her famle
and the ~~ea~~ colors
pink and purple
and tlue and black
✗ She rele likes
her bab and her
mom not rile he
bruthrs and her frends
ane Gracie and Lizsy

Emma

this morning
wen I was woking
I chript and my
sistr helpt me
up.

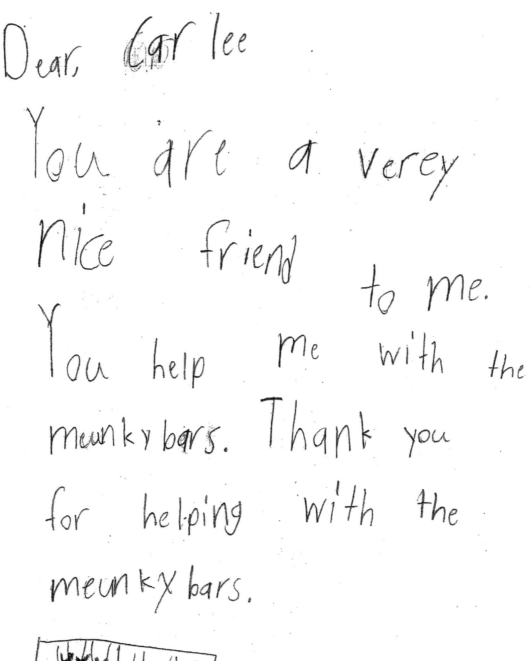

Dear, Carlee

You are a verey
nice friend
to me.
You help me with the
meunky bars. Thank you
for helping with the
meunky bars.

Sincerly, Ivy

Name: Michael J

Dear Heros thank
you for fighting
for our freedom
and our city and
country and
keeping us safe.
It makes me feel
Good.   From, Michael J

Liyos
Liyons
for
Liyons
gral
Liyons
run
Lixons
sleep
Lixons
snor
Lixons

Fall levs
by Delilah
Red levs bumpy rough
blowing off the trees
Piling in there own piles
in the corner of the fencs
Just to Jump in!

Space Report
What I saw

- Saturn's Rings
- Stars
- Clouds - (Zoomed In)
- ~~Saturn's Ring~~ Saturn's Rings' Gas
- ~~Asteroid~~ Comet
- Color changing Rings - probably gas lines.
- Comet trails
- Saturn's Moons
- Big Gasses

What I Found Out

- There's lot's of gasses out there in space.

- Some Stars are out - Probably when they're getting old - stars have a life span!

Date _____

Dear _____

I'm so excited to share my story with you! I've spent a lot of time working on it in school, coming up with an idea to write about, sharing it aloud, planning my story, writing it, and sharing it with my classmates to make it better and better. Now I have a story I'm proud of. I hope you enjoy reading it!

Please take a minute to write me a quick note telling me what you liked about my story. It doesn't have to be long—just a few sentences would be great. This will further encourage me to continue writing.

Thank you so much!
Sincerely,

_____

Date _____

Dear _____

I'm so excited to share my story with you! I've spent a lot of time working on it in school, coming up with an idea to write about, sharing it aloud, planning my story, writing it, and sharing it with my classmates to make it better and better. Now I have a story I'm proud of. I hope you enjoy reading it!

Please take a minute to write me a quick note telling me what you liked about my story. It doesn't have to be long—just a few sentences would be great. This will further encourage me to continue writing.

Thank you so much!
Sincerely,

_____

More Strategies for Using Mentor Texts in Your Classroom

CRAFT MOVES
Lesson Sets for Teaching Writing with Mentor Texts
Stacey Shubitz
Foreword by Lester Laminack

DREAM WAKERS
Mentor Texts That Celebrate Latino Culture
Ruth Culham
Foreword by Pam Muñoz Ryan

THE WRITING THIEF
Using Mentor Texts to Teach the Craft of Writing
Ruth Culham

NONFICTION MENTOR TEXTS
Teaching Informational Writing Through Children's Literature, K–8
Lynne R. Dorfman and Rose Cappelli
Foreword by Tony Stead

Also available: *Mentor Texts, Second Edition,* and *Poetry Mentor Texts*

For Product Safety Concerns and Information please contact our EU
representative GPSR@taylorandfrancis.com Taylor & Francis Verlag GmbH,
Kaufingerstraße 24, 80331 München, Germany

Printed and bound by CPI Group (UK) Ltd, Croydon, CR0 4YY
08/06/2025
01897012-0002